My Mother's Child

. . . vignettes from the life of a "little greek girl"

By

Stella C. Hatgiannis

To Kimberly -
Thanks for sharing my
special evening —
Stella H.
1/16/04

ISBN: 1-4140-2082-1 (e-book)
ISBN: 1-4140-2081-3 (Paperback)

This book is printed on acid free paper.

1stBooks - rev. 11/11/03

My womb mate, my soul mate, my twin, died after one day on this earth. Together for nine months and suddenly he was gone, leaving me to face life on earth alone. And so my life began, alone, fighting for my very existence.

I was to become the all to my parents, their shining star, their hope of the future, their link to each other and theirs to mold into what they perceived I should be.

Alone, I accepted the burdens placed on my young shoulders. Alone, I fought my battles, winning some and losing many. Alone, I survived my father's death. Alone, I became my mother's anchor. Alone I survived loneliness, assumed responsibilities beyond my years. Alone I cared for my mother through the years, coping with the difficulties of watching a loved one age, deteriorate and slowly ease towards death. I did it all.....alone.

I write these stories, these fragments of memory, to bring closure to the past, to better understand myself and to appreciate my parents' efforts. They lived and loved as best they knew how. I am a result of their efforts, but I alone take responsibility for what I have become.

HOW IT ALL STARTED....

left to right- Maria, Christos, Charles 1920

LETTER FROM A STRANGER

Poverty had settled over the small Greek village, a smothering, festering vapor that spared no one. There was no escape; it was for all to share.

The devastation of the latest attack was visible as far as one could see. Houses had been reduced to roofless cubes. Rubble disfigured the rolling hills and countryside. Olive trees, once rich and fruitful, stretched barren limbs to the sky as if seeking forgiveness. Birds no longer twittered and flowers no longer bloomed. Only the pitiful meow of a lost kitten or a whimper of a wounded dog broke the silence.

Old men shuffled along the dirt road leading to nowhere in a desperate search for cronies from the coffee shop - the *cafenion* - that no longer existed. Women sat on broken steps cuddling infants vainly seeking food at empty breasts. Children with the endless stamina and innocence of youth ran up and down the heaps of rubble, fabricating war games and wounding imaginary enemy soldiers.

This was Adramit, Turkey, 1922.

Costandina shaded her eyes against the rising sun as she climbed the path to the village square in search of water. She walked quickly, swinging the battered pails in monotonous rhythm. "Good morning," she muttered as she passed her neighbors.

"Good morning, Mrs. Costandina." She was highly regarded in the village hierarchy and the formal salutation was given as a matter of respect. Mrs. Costandina, rarely Costandina.

"How did you sleep?" she would ask, never stopping for a reply. Her quest for water was urgent and idle chatter would come later. She soon reached the well and silently prayed that it would provide the nourishing water. It was still early and she was the first to reach the well this day.

Costandina leaned over the side of the well and peered down into the murky darkness. She threw a pebble into the well and waited for its descent. She bent closer to the edge of the well, not daring to breathe or move until she heard the splash. The pebble tumbled downwards and the comforting sounds of its arrival signaled Costandina to begin drawing the water.

She grasped the worn rope handles of the two buckets, carefully balancing their weight against her body. Costandina was a small woman but her stature disguised the wiry strength within. The buckets swayed back and forth, hitting her thighs with each step as she made her way homeward.

The sun climbed higher. Blistering rays pointed their way downward towards the little village. Another scorching day with no relief until sunset. Only then would they feel the breeze from the sea and cool their burning bodies. Costandina rested halfway home, lowering the buckets onto the rocky path. She sat on a pile of broken stones and fanned her flushed face with her apron. She was tempted to dip her fingers into the buckets and soothe her burning cheeks with the cool water. But she did not.

Costandina arrived at the shell of a house and sighed as she remembered better days. It was home for the six of them, but one with half a roof and little furniture. She kicked the door open as she smiled to herself. A door? What use was a door when there was only half a roof? The door banged against the stucco wall, releasing a battered board from the frame, sending it skittering across the floor. "Oh, well," Costandina sighed, "one more stick for firewood."

She adjusted her eyes to the dim interior as she lowered the buckets near the washstand. There they would stay, closely guarded. Portions would be doled out as needed. Two trips a week to the well were all that they were allowed and the precious liquid was not to be wasted.

"Maria," shouted Costandina. "Maria, come here. Where are you?"

A stirring in the far corner alerted her to Maria's presence. She walked across the tile floor and stood in front of Maria where she sat by the battered wood stove stirring a copper pot. "Oh, mamma, I'm here. I've been up a long time. I'm warming milk for breakfast. Do you want some?"

Costandina knew how much Maria loved to sleep in the morning and she doubted Maria's early rising. "A long time, eh? Where did you get the milk? Where is Athena? Where are the boys? You're the mother when I'm not here. You should know where they are."

Maria sighed and continued stirring. "I sent Charles to the neighbors. Their goat is finally giving milk and I traded some bread for milk." She smiled at her ingenuity and waited for her mother's praise.

"The bread? You gave the bread away? That was to last us for two more days!" shrieked Costandina.

Maria stepped back in fright. She had never seen her mother so enraged. "But … but I got us some milk. We now have milk, enough for two days," she sobbed. Tears streamed down her thin and colorless cheeks.

Costandina walked towards the table and picked up the clay pitcher filled with milk. She calculated its contents. With the milk, flour borrowed from a neighbor and the sugar and yeast she had managed to save, she would bake a few loaves of nourishing and filling bread.

Maria gently wiped her face with the small handkerchief she kept in her dress pocket. It was tattered and dingy but it had once been her favorite. She had managed to salvage it during the storming of the village only because it had been in the pocket of her dress. She began to smooth the small patch of linen, carefully tracing the flowers embroidered in each corner. She patted the torn creamy lace around the edges as she gently folded it and placed it back in her pocket for safekeeping. It was the only beautiful belonging she had left.

Costandina sighed as she looked at her forlorn daughter. “Don’t burn the milk. Pour it into the bowls. I hear the boys coming.”

Six chipped bowls were arranged around the table. Maria poured equal amounts in each. She wanted no arguments today. She was tired of complaints and tired of being the second mother. Poverty was hard and she knew she had to do her best to help Costandina. They had never been deprived of food and clothing, even after her father’s death. Costandina had managed to provide the five children with clean clothes, ample food and a comfortable home. That had changed virtually overnight with no warning. Everyone was in the same predicament now. Sharing and trading were prevalent but no one had much more than a neighbor did. Maria sighed, swallowed hard and composed herself before saying a prayer of thanks. They began the morning meal.

Days came and went in monotonous sameness. The village struggled to restore life to some semblance of normalcy. It was Saturday and supper was finished. Dishes were washed and dried and put away. Maria walked out into the coolness of the small garden and sat on the splintered wooden bench under the lemon tree. Christos, her older brother, walked out and joined her. He lit a cigarette that he had been rationing for several days. He sighed and leaned against the brittle bark of the old tree, blowing smoke rings into the air. They stared out into the silent evening lost in their own thoughts.

The garden was no longer beautiful. It was nothing more than tangled weeds now. The lemon tree was barren. The grass was scorched and littered with bits of broken flowerpots. Maria looked up through the tangled, empty branches and remembered summers past when the scent of lemons wafted through the yard and into the house. She remembered the abundance of lemons as large as oranges. She remembered climbing the tree and gathering lemons in a fast race against her brothers. She remembered and she wept. “Oh, Christos,” she wailed. “What are we going to do? I don’t know what more I can do to help. What is mamma going to do with all of us? There are too many mouths to feed.”

Christos squeezed his eyes shut against the sight of his weeping sister. Her anguish was real but so was the reality of the village. He had reluctantly joined the army and he was at least assured of food and clothing. Charles was eking out a meager existence as a tailor's apprentice which provided a few coins towards the family's food. Stefanos would join the navy as soon as he finished school. Athena was still considered the baby of the family, but as all young girls she was learning to knit and embroider. Christos realized that only Maria lacked a plan. She was too young to be so burdened and too old to be single.

Christos sighed in relief as the solution to the problem of Maria came to him. He would find a husband for his sister. He opened his eyes and slyly scrutinized Maria as she sat beside him. She was small in stature like Costandina. She was gentle but with a backbone of steel. Her lustrous black hair, once cut in a stylish bob, was now pulled back and tied with a scrap of cloth. Her eyes were dark as midnight and ringed with double rows of lashes. He had never really noticed that before; how remarkable were her eyes. Her nose was straight and classic. Her once rounded cheeks were slightly sunken and colorless but a proper diet would remedy this. But she was twenty years old, too old by village standards to be single. Not her fault, of course. All able-bodied young men had been drafted or forced into military service. Others had abandoned the village in desperate escape plans to seek a better life elsewhere. Many had been killed by the invaders. The village now consisted of women, children and old men. He had to find a husband for Maria, somehow, somewhere.

1923

The sun slid behind the distant mountains to its bed of rest. The moon slipped into the night sky and stars sent their silvery sparks earthward. Stillness and darkness softened the harshness of the village. Neighbors slowly emerged to seek the cooling breeze which arrived every evening. Costandina swept the broken steps and carefully spread a burlap bag over the top step. She lowered herself onto the step, folding the voluminous folds of her dress about her. "Ahhhh," she sighed. "Ahhhhh, we forget for a while and enjoy the coolness of the night."

Summer shifted slowly into an early fall. The scorched earth eagerly awaited the September rains. Children prepared reluctantly for school. Mothers counted the days until the arrival of the teacher. The schoolhouse had been cleared of debris and scrubbed clean by the village women. Books, papers and pencils had been salvaged from the aftermath of the pillaging. Desks had been repaired and chairs nailed together. There would be school for the children.

Costandina walked slowly on her way home from the village marketplace. Shopping for the day's meal had been successful. She shifted the baskets into a more comfortable position and continued along the rocky path. She pondered the fate of her family. With scrimping and saving and great ingenuity, Costandina provided food, clothing and shelter. Her greatest concern, however, was Maria. Other village girls had grasped at marriage offers eagerly but Maria remained stubborn and difficult.

Young men returning to the village faced poverty and few opportunities. Although they yearned for families of their own, providing for parents came first. Restoring the village and recouping family prosperity were top priorities. The young men eyed Maria longingly as she went back and forth to the village. She secretly enjoyed the attention and flirtations but marriage was not yet likely. It seemed a hopeless situation.

Reaching her destination, Costandina placed the grocery baskets on the broken steps and sat on the concrete step still warm from the afternoon sun. Christos soon joined her and mother and son communed in silence as the afternoon shadows lengthened.

Christos finally broke the silence. "Mamma," he began, "I want to say something. Money is a big worry for you. I know how hard it is for you to keep us fed and clothed. I know you worry about Maria. I do, too. Her sewing does bring in some money but she has to think of the future - hers, yours and even ours. Charles and Stefanos and I will want to get married someday but we can't until she's married, you know that. If she waits much longer, no one will want her - or us!" He quickly gave his mother a smile to lessen the gravity of his statement. "I'll think of someone or something to do, mamma, I will!"

"What great ideas do you have?" Costandina asked. "Even Mrs. Penelope can't help. She visited yesterday with more names of marriage prospects but I'm afraid to tell Maria."

Christos shuddered remembering Mrs. Penelope's last visit. As the self-appointed village matchmaker, mothers and daughters welcomed her visits. Not so Maria. Last month, Mrs. Penelope had presented Costandina with a list of names for Maria's consideration. Maria had shrieked at the thought of marrying any of the suitors on Mrs. Penelope's list. She vowed to remain a spinster forever before giving herself to any of them. Costandina, flushed with embarrassment, had quickly escorted Mrs. Penelope out, apologizing for her ungrateful daughter. Christos knew another visit from Mrs. Penelope would be worse than the last. Another course of action had to be found.

A few days later, a soft knock on the door broke the silence of the afternoon. Costandina made her way to the door, quickly wiping her hands free of bread dough. Flour was becoming available and baking bread was now almost a daily chore. She opened the door and found Olga, a friend and neighbor, standing on the threshold. "Come in, come in," she said. "I'll put the coffee pot on; the bread will be done soon. Welcome."

Olga shuffled her vast body into the tidy living room. She gazed at the meager furnishings and selected the sturdiest of the chairs to sit on. "Ahhh, thank you, Mrs. Costandina, thank you. I haven't seen you for a while. You look well. I hope you are managing? These are very tough times for all of us," she said, emphasizing her observations with a huge sigh.

"What can I tell you, Olga," responded Costandina. "It is very hard but I thank God for my family. We manage."

"And how is Maria? I haven't seen her lately. Perhaps she is engaged?"

"Ah, from your lips to God's ears, Mrs. Olga. No, no, Maria is here. She works for Mrs. Calipso, learning to be a dressmaker. She's very good, lots of talent. Where she got it, I don't know," she laughed. "Some of the wealthy ladies in town are beginning to ask her to sew for them. I'm proud of her, but I'm worried too."

Olga murmured agreement. "Yes, yes, I know," she sighed. "My daughter was the same, too independent. But she's married now. She has two - two! babies now." She folded her arms over her ample chest and smiled smugly at her daughter's good fortune.

"Mrs. Costandina," began Olga. "I have a thought. See what you think. My cousin … he's in America now. He's alone over there. His mother, father, brothers - they were all killed the last time." She sighed and wiped a large tear as it rolled down her plump cheek. "Terrible; terrible. He got to America just in time, thank God." She stopped and murmured a prayer for the souls of her departed relatives. "His name is Christos," she began again. "Christos, just like your son. You remember his mother, Ralia? His father, Yanni? From the next village. You met them, I know. They would visit me often. Very nice people. May their souls rest in peace." She wiped another tear and sighed.

"America? That's so far away!" Costandina observed. "America? What does he do there? How would he and Maria ever meet? Impossible." She paused. "America, eh? He must have money. Is he rich?"

Olga pondered these perplexing questions. She knew little of life in America for Christos. He wrote infrequent letters which said little but conveyed so much. He was lonely, frightened and guilty. He was lonely with no family and few friends. He was frightened of living in a strange county and learning its new ways. He felt guilty for escaping to America while his mother, father and brothers were buried in unknown graves. His only surviving relative was Olga. Letters to her were his only link to the village and life as he had known it.

a family gathering in Adramit – my paternal grandparents

"He asked me in his last letter to find him a wife," continued Olga. She glanced at Costandina to gauge her reaction to this bit of news.

Frowning, Costandina pulled her chair closer to Olga. "He wants a wife? From here? They don't have women in America?" she huffed.

Olga laughed. Poor Costandina, how naive and unworldly she was. "Of course there are women in America," began Olga patiently. "There are many women but there are not many Greek women."

"What can you do for him? He's in America, thousand of miles from here. Tell him to come here and look for himself. If he wants a Greek girl, he must come here."

With that, Costandina stood up, indicating that the conversation had ended. Olga sipped the last of her coffee and carefully set the cup on the table. The dainty cup was chipped and cracked. It was the only one left from a set of twelve. Olga knew how much Costandina loved fine things and it was sad to see her friend struggling to maintain her dignity. Olga rose and placed an arm around Costandina's thin shoulders. "Costandina - and I now call you Costandina, not Mrs. Costandina - I am your friend and I will help in any way I can. I don't have much to offer but my friendship. We'll talk again soon, agree? Think about what I just told you." She hugged her friend and left without another word.

Evening approached as daylight struggled to filter its last rays through the gray clouds. Maria was on her way home after another tiring day. Sewing beautiful dresses for others was neither exciting nor very profitable. Her eyes burned from straining at tiny stitches and her fingers hurt from needle pricks. She thought of the few dollars she was bringing home. Most would be spent for food and what remained Costandina would place into Maria's dowry fund. Maria's sad face lit up as she thought of her dowry and she slid a few coins into a hiding place in her sewing basket. She had her secret fund for dreams of material, ribbons, laces and fancy buttons.

Maria walked quickly into the kitchen and kissed her mother's cheek, pushing a wayward wisp of hair away from her forehead as she did so. Costandina was warm from the glow of the wood stove and the scent of smoke was in her hair. Maria hugged her and placed her week's wages in Costandina's outstretched hand. "See, mamma, I'm getting more work and more money." Costandina smiled and stuffed the hard-earned wages in her apron pocket. She patted Maria gently on the cheek and pushed her out of the way.

Christos, Charles and Stefanos arrived and chaos descended. They were a rowdy group, full of teasing and joking. Costandina reminded them to settle down and wash up for supper. Athena worked her way around the table, setting out the plates as she had been taught. Maria placed a bowl of rice in the center of the table. Steam rose in wispy curls towards the ceiling. The aroma of sweet butter melting over the mound of rice enticed their appetites. They hurriedly gathered around the table. A chicken had been slaughtered that morning. It was a tough bird but smothered in onions and tomato sauce, heavily spiced and cooked for hours had produced a meal fit for a king by Costandina's standards. "Eat, eat, before it gets cold," she warned as her family was fed for yet another day. Costandina silently prayed for continued abundance.

November. Cold and darkness were endured with thoughts of holidays and better days to come. The family had survived the difficult months. Life was improving and they were thriving. Costandina glanced out of the cracked window and saw Mihali, the postman, coming up the path towards the house. The heavy mailbag was slung over his shoulder, pounding his back with every step he took over the rocky path. She scurried to the stove to put the coffeepot on in preparation for Mihali's visit. He often stopped to rest and visit with Costandina and she welcomed his visits and the news of the village. She opened the door before he had a chance to knock and ushered him in.

"Mrs. Costandina, good morning. I smelled the coffee and I thank you in advance." He eased himself onto the chair by the table, dropping the heavy bag at his feet and waited to be served the pungent coffee. "I have a letter here for you. No, no, not for you, I see, but for Maria." He pulled out an envelope with great flourish. "Here, see, it says, 'To Mademoiselle Maria ."

Costandina snatched the letter from his hand. Who would be writing to Maria? She ripped the envelope and pulled out a thin sheet of paper covered with scrawling words in black ink.

Costandina cursed. She cried. She lamented this intrusion. "Olga went behind my back," she shouted at Mihali, the unsuspecting messenger. "What am I going to do with this letter?"

Mihali was at a loss as to what had provoked such agitation. "Mrs. Costandina, calm down. Your face is red and your eyes are ready to pop out. Give me that letter." He reached for Costandina's hand but she was much too quick. She pushed the letter deep into her apron pocket.

"It's nothing, Mihali, nothing. Just a joke Olga is playing on me. Here, have more coffee, Mihali, before you go. It's very cold outside."

That night Costandina waited until everyone was asleep. She crept quietly into the kitchen. She lit the oil lamp and sat by the wood stove absorbing the last gusts of warmth. She eased the crinkled letter from its smudged and torn envelope. She smoothed out the creases of the tissue-thin paper. She bent forward closer to the light and to the warmth. She began to read.

"Dear Mademoiselle: I am Christos, from America. I write to you on advice of my cousin Olga, who has spoken with your brother. I hope you don't mind. I know of your family and I'm sure your family knows of mine and all that has happened. I do not know you and you do not know me. I hope you won't think I am too bold. I am lonely in a strange country and would like you to write to me. With many best wishes to you and your family, I remain, your fellow countryman, Christos."

Costandina crumbled the letter in her fist. The nerve! The audacity! Did he think her daughter was desperate? Did he think she would sacrifice her daughter to a stranger? What had Olga told him? Maria must never know of this letter. She placed it back in her pocket and shuffled off to bed.

Costandina left the house early the next morning in an effort to avoid her family. She was on her way to the market, deep in thought. Suddenly she felt someone nudge her arm. She blinked and brought herself out of her stupor and into the crisp cold air of the sunless morning.

"Good morning, Mrs.Costandina. How are you today?" trilled Olga. "Any news to tell me?"

Costandina continued pushing her way through the crowd of early morning shoppers and vendors, hoping to lose Olga. Despite her bulk, Olga soon caught up with Costandina and pulled her to a stop. "Don't pretend you don't know what I'm asking," huffed Olga. "What do you think?" she wheezed.

"What do I think?" hissed Costandina. "What do I think? What were you thinking? This Christos must be a pervert and you are to blame!"

"My dear friend Costandina, listen to me. I watch Maria come and go, back and forth to the houses of the rich to sew their dresses. She's a pretty girl but the freshness of this young flower is dimming. She is sad. She wants to live but she sees the futility of her dreams. What do you want her to do? Wither on the vine? Where are the grooms-to-be here? What are you doing for her? Nothing but sucking the life out of her."

Olga gasped at what she had just said. Surely this would be the end of their friendship.

Costandina resumed walking through the marketplace as Olga ran to catch up with her. Costandina stopped abruptly as Olga collided into her. Costandina pushed Olga away and shouted, "You blame me? Me? I've struggled for years without my husband to keep everyone together. I want the best for Maria but there is nothing here. What more can I do? You want me to sacrifice her to a stranger? No, I won't do that!"

"My friend, dear Costandina," began Olga in a low soothing tone. "Calm down. I think of Maria as I do of my own daughter. I want her to have a chance at life and a family of her own. Do you want any less for her? Do you have any better ideas, you who knows it all?"

Costandina resumed her pace, with Olga beside her. They walked in silence as Costandina pondered the future of her daughter. She reluctantly agreed that Olga was right, but how could Costandina accept the intrusion of a stranger? But what other choices were there? Maria was but one of many young women waiting for suitable marriages. The fear of another attack on the village, the threat of pillaging, plundering and raping was always a threat over their heads. She must think of Maria's future.

"Olga," she began, "I'll ask Maria. I can't speak for her. She will be the one to decide."

Olga grinned and hugged her friend. "You're doing the right thing, I know you are." With that, she kissed her friend on the cheek and whispered that everything would be all right.

That evening the crumbled letter was placed on the kitchen table. Olga smoothed the creased page with her callused hands. She read it once more. She studied it, analyzing each word, trying to bring about the reality of this stranger, this Christos from America.

Maria glanced at her mother as she passed by. She noticed the piece of paper in Costandina's hand and stopped. She bent forward to get a closer look but Costandina quickly folded the paper to hide its contents. "What's that?" Maria asked. "Who wrote you a letter?" The arrival of a letter usually meant bad news. "Who died?"

"Sit down," Costandina ordered. "Sit down next to me."

"But mamma, it's time to eat. I have to serve the food. Athena is already whining; Christos is due in from camp and the others will be here soon."

"Supper will wait. I have something to show you."

Maria pulled up a chair next to her mother and gazed into her eyes. "What is it, mamma? What bad news do you have?"

"I don't know if it is bad or good. You will decide." She thrust the letter into Maria's hand and waited.

Maria's hands trembled. She had never received a letter before. There was no one who could possibly be writing to her. She frowned as she carefully unfolded the wrinkled page and began to read.

"Dear Mademoiselle: I am Christos, Christos from America …."

WHEN MARIA MET CHRISTOS

March, 1927

Maria shivered as she stood on the dock. The raw March wind blew fiercely, sending debris swirling against her ankles and flying into her eyes. She clutched the collar of her new coat a little tighter and closed her eyes against the icy gusts.

The foghorn at the Port of Piraeus suddenly shrieked. It was time to board. Maria turned, blinking back tears, some from the wind, most from emotions she was trying to conceal. She walked a few steps forward to where her mother and brother stood chatting with Christos, her new husband. The enormity of the day's events suddenly overwhelmed her, dizzied her, frightened her. Who was this man, this stranger? Three years of corresponding had not prepared her for the real flesh and blood of him. Three years' worth of letters crossing the ocean to America and back, three days of hurried wedding preparations and three hours of marriage. What was she doing here? Who was he?

Her mother hugged her tightly, kissing her and caressing her, murmuring, "My child, my child; when will my eyes ever see you again?".

Stefanos, Maria's younger brother, walked towards them, the gold buttons on his naval uniform catching the last rays of the sun. His military training was now coming into good use; no emotional display, no feelings disclosed; just the reality of the moment to be dealt with. He gently pulled mother and daughter apart, pushing himself between them and guided them to the gangplank and the waiting ship. He slapped his new brother-in-law heartily on the shoulder in a manly display of bravado and jokingly wished Christos good luck with Maria, his "rotten older sister." Christos smiled and enveloped him in a bear hug as he quickly slipped a few hard-earned American dollars into Stefanos's coat pocket as a parting gesture to a newly-acquired brother-in-law and a newfound friend. Christos shyly kissed his mother-in-law and gently pried Maria from her side. Tears streamed down their faces, mingling with the rain that was now misting around them. The foghorn blasted again. Final hugs and kisses were traded. Maria and Christos began the slow ascent up the gangplank to the upper deck. Maria was filled with many emotions. She was leaving her family, her friends, her homeland. She was sailing off to a strange land with no knowledge of its language and customs. She was no longer the idolized older daughter and sister. She was now a wife, facing unknown challenges, joys and hardships. Could she do it? Would she?

The murky waters swirled below them. One last blast from the foghorn and they were on their way. The journey had begun. Maria raised her right hand, waving frantically to her mother and brother standing below at dockside. Christos pulled her closer to him and bent down to wipe the tears from her face.

my mother

my father

"Hello, Maria, I'm Christos; Christos from America," he said with a wide grin.

She turned and looking up at Christos, smiled and shyly offered her hand - and her heart - to him. A new life awaited her.

left to right- Christos, Maria, Stefanos Going to America
1927

My parents, Maria and Christos, settled in Reading, Pennsylvania, joining many other Greek immigrants who had fled the villages in Turkey and now sought a better life in America.

Life was hard. The men worked in factories and the women cooked, cleaned, baked, had babies and kept the family unit strong. They sought comfort from each other as they had no one else. They struggled to learn English and tried to blend in with their new homeland. Families in Turkey were never heard from again and strangers were now family.

My mother gave birth to a son, John, in 1928. Their hopes and dreams were personified by this child. They were establishing a home and family of their own and life in America was good.

However, their happiness was short-lived. Baby John died twenty-months later and they were devastated. Torn apart from family in Turkey, with only new friends to offer comfort, they struggled to overcome their grief. My father immersed himself in work and evenings at the "cafenion", the coffeehouse, commiserating with cronies over strong coffee and poor poker hands. My mother occupied herself with housework and the neighbors and vowed never to have another child. There had been too many losses in her life and she could not bear another.

But that was soon to change.

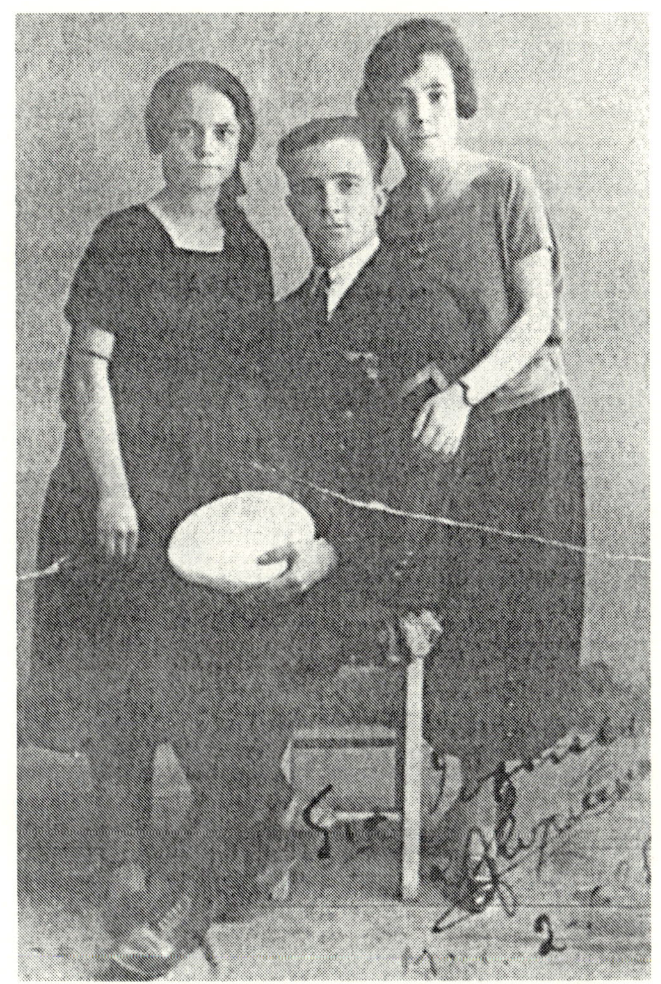

left to right- Athena, Stefanos, Maria 1925

READING, PENNSYLVANIA 1932 - 1937

first picture in America

my favorite photo of my parents

Christos (left), Maria (right), baby John, first-born son (center)

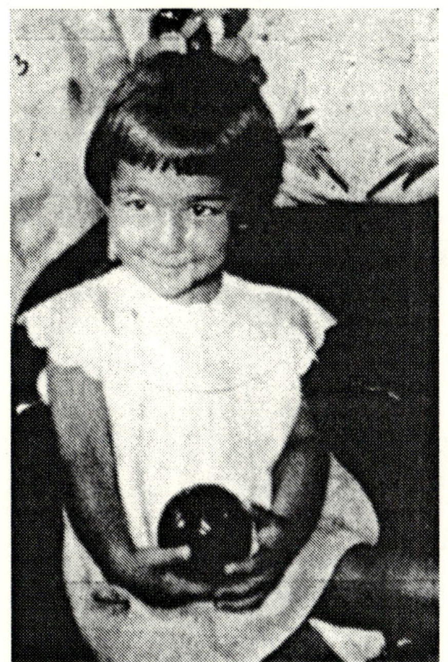

Stella

OH, BROTHER!

January 8, 1932

It was a battle, this waiting to be born. For nine months he had fought for womb space a twin sister was not willing to share. For nine months he had given in to her flailing arms and flapping legs. For nine months he had been pushed around by this sister-to-be. But no more! It was time to be born and he had decided he was not going to be the first. He wanted to enjoy space of his own, even for a little while. She would have to go.

The walls of the womb pushed, pulled and pummeled the two of them. His sister looked at him with frightened eyes as she was bounced and hurled around the confines of their place of hibernation. He positioned himself next to her. His legs pushed against her back, sending her plummeting downward and outward. He stretched and savored the silence and the space until it was time for him to plunge forward.

"Oh, it's a boy! Oh, how cute!" he heard as he made his entrance into the waiting world of blinding lights and overwhelming sounds. He felt gentle hands wiping his body, clearing his eyes, wrapping him in warm, snug blankets. He whimpered at the commotion around him. He nuzzled against the warm body holding him.

"Look, look," he heard, "he's sure ready to eat!" Plump arms held him closer and he burrowed deeper into the confines of the ample body.

"I'm taking him to his mom," he heard. He clung tightly to the nursery attendant as she made her way down the long corridor, the stiff starched uniform rustling, the rubber-soled shoes squeaking with every step.

"Here we are, honey," she announced as she pushed the door forward and entered a darkened room. “Here’s your mommy,” she said as she patted his freshly powdered and diapered round bottom.

Soft arms soon cradled him. A cooing voice murmured sweet sounds into his ear. Warm butterfly kisses caressed his face. He squirmed and sought warmth. He snuggled and found food. He nestled into a safe haven. He was content.

Suddenly a wail pierced the silence. His ears resonated with echoes of discord. He blinked his eyes to better see the source of this turmoil. He turned his head to focus on the cause of this disturbance.

He noticed a bundle next to him. A wiggling, squirming bundle of pink blankets was trying to displace him. He snuggled deeper, fighting for his territorial rights, clinging to the arms encircling him. He peeked at a tiny wrinkled face surrounded by pink blankets. The eyes were tightly shut, the mouth wide open as the wailing continued and arms waved wildly in protest.

He felt a kick, then another. A fist brushed by his face. The pink bundle was in full battle mode. It was his sister! Once again she was fighting for space she felt she deserved. He retreated deeper into the folds of the blankets, defenseless before this frantic fury of a female child.

“Here, here, baby boy,” a voice murmured. “Let’s take you back to the nursery until she’s finished eating.” He was back in the plump circle of the attendant’s arms heading towards the nursery bassinet while the pink bundled sister staked her claim.

The door swung open into the nursery. The wails, murmurs and cries of the tiny inhabitants blended into a cacophony of sounds, a symphony of discontent. He was placed gently into the waiting bassinet as soft, warm, fluffy blankets were layered over him.

“This one’s the cute twin,” he heard.

“Yeah; he’s quiet, too,” another voice chimed in. “That girl baby is a holy terror already."

He smiled as he thought of his sister. He drifted off to sleep.

They never saw each other again.

****

This is how I envision my birth and my twin brother's death. This is how I became my mother's child.

Understandably, my parents hovered over me, over-protected me and smothered me with love and kindness and almost everything I ever wanted. I relate now some childhood stories - instances that drove my mother to the brink, I'm sure!

Stella – 7 months old

BUBBLEGUM, PEANUTS AND LOLLIPOPS

I remember that bubblegum was my favorite purchase from the corner candy store. I would chew and chomp and blow bubbles until my jaws ached. My five-cent weekly allowance, plus the five cents Kally's poppa gave all of us kids on the block from his weekly pay envelope, provided me with all the gum and candy I wanted.

My baby teeth were falling out at a fast pace. Daily, momma warned me not to chew gum or eat caramels in case I swallowed a loose tooth. But nothing would stop me.

I continued my weekly stop at the candy store, filling up two small paper bags with candy and gum. I occasionally shared with my friends but mostly I kept it all for myself. Bubble-blowing was a contest in the neighborhood and I was perfecting my talents.

Then catastrophe struck. Caramel and baby tooth went sliding down to my tummy. I was scared, not knowing what would happen once the tooth landed in my stomach. I had to tell momma.

Momma eased my fears. However, a warning was issued that I was not to chew bubblegum or eat caramels until all the baby teeth had been replaced. Momma confiscated my piggy bank, leaving me with no candy allowance.

A few days later, I was sitting on the bottom front porch step, sunning myself. I hummed happily as I bounced a little red rubber ball on the sidewalk. Life was good. Momma came out and smiled at me, content that I was amusing myself and not bothering her while she was cleaning house. She turned to go back into the house but looked back one more time. There I sat with a huge pink bubblegum bubble ready to explode in my face.

"Stella," she shouted. "I told you not to buy bubblegum. You're ruining your teeth." She stepped down to the pavement and watched in horror as the bubble grew to immense proportions and then exploded. “Where did you get that? You have no money.”

I looked up at her, pink bubblegum splattered all over my face. “I found it,” I said, gloating in my success.

“Found it? Where? Who gave it to you?”

“Nobody. I found it. There,” I said, pointing to the sidewalk. “I found it there and scraped it up…with this.” I pointed at another found treasure, a discarded piece of a rusted nail file.

There went the logic to momma’s lectures about germs, eating off of someone else’s plate and picking up food that dropped to the floor. She had never mentioned sidewalks!

****

It was a crisp November day. Leaves had turned to gold and red, ending up in raked piles for us to jump into and run through, giggling wildly in our pleasure.

Momma and I were walking home after a quick stop at the grocery store. It was almost time for daddy to come home and momma still had to fix dinner. As we reached the corner, I spotted the roasted peanuts vendor. I broke loose from momma’s tight grip and ran to Mr. Steve, waving wildly to get his attention. The peanuts were packed in little brown paper bags, ready for sale. They were warm and smelled so delicious. I wanted some. “Hi, Mr. Steve,” I chirped. “I want some peanuts.”

Momma found a nickel at the bottom of her purse and handed it over to Mr. Steve. He opened a bag and poured extra peanuts into it. He twisted it shut and handed it to me, smiling at my evident joy. I took the bag between my mittened hands and smiled my thanks and waved goodbye.

I ate as we continued our way home, scattering peanut shells along the way. I cracked them open and ate the little peanuts, still toasty warm. Momma smiled at my delight.

We were almost home when momma stopped to talk to Mr. Pete, our next-door neighbor. I stood quietly by momma's side while she and Mr. Pete talked. I grew impatient as I wanted to continue eating my peanuts, but they kept talking and talking.

Mr. Pete glanced down at me and saw me clutching the paper bag. "Ahhh," he said, "I see you bought some peanuts from Mr. Steve."

I nodded and clutched the paper bag even tighter.

"So," he continued, "could I have some? They smell so good."

Fear struck my heart. This meant I would have to share. I looked up at him and gazed directly into his eyes.

"No; these are just the peanut shells. I ate them all."

Momma's mouth gaped open in surprise. She whispered, "I'm sorry," to Mr. Pete as she grabbed my arm and quickly made our way home. She was so ashamed.

I continued to crack open the peanuts, slowly devouring them, one by one.

****

A Saturday afternoon in May. My friends and I were sprawled on the front porch of Kally's house, not knowing what to do. Our repertoire of games had been exhausted. It was too soon for the ice cream wagon and too late for a raid on the ice house. We were totally bored.

The sun jumped from cloud to cloud, sending sunbeams and shadows as it played hide and seek. Reed Street was quiet. All the mommas were busy with cooking and cleaning. Daddies were at the neighborhood coffee house reading newspapers and playing cards.

Everyone had something to do except us.

I noticed the parked cars on either side of Reed Street. A few of the neighbors down the street now had cars and parked them proudly along the curb. They were washed and waxed every Saturday, ready for the family outings on Sunday. Most cars had a radio antenna on the side, topped with a colored glass bead. I started walking up the street looking at the shiny beads and marveling at the many different colors. They were made of clear glass - red, blue, yellow, green - even black. They were like little lollipops gleaming in the sparse sunlight.

Lollipops! I would pretend they were lollipops! I ran up one side of the street and the other "tasting" each lollipop, licking accumulated dust and dirt off of the glass beads, savoring their imaginary flavors.

How wonderful to be so young, imaginative and carefree!

My mother was the disciplinarian, since she was home every day to witness my many shortcomings. My father worked long, late hours and time with him was precious. I knew I could provoke my mother only so far, but I didn't dare (usually) disturb my father's tranquillity. But there were times.....

FOOD FOR THOUGHT

It was time for Sunday dinner, but I was too busy playing with my dolls to stop. Momma called and called again. I continued playing.

She came into the playroom and snatched the dolls from my hands. She pulled me upright from the floor and slowly led me downstairs to the kitchen.

The table was set and daddy was already seated at the head of the table. He motioned for me to sit down at my usual place. A delicious aroma bubbled up from the big pot on the stove as momma filled our plates and brought them to the table.

I looked at the food placed before me. I looked at momma and quickly announced, "I "
don't like it."

"What don't you like?" she asked. "Try it; it's good for you."

"What's in it? What's that stuff? I don't like it," I repeated.

"You've never had it before, so how do you know?"

"I know!"

"Stella, it is lamb with celery and a nice hollandaise sauce. It's very good. Try it."

"No," I said.

"Hrrmph," sounded daddy. "Hrrmph."

I looked at him. He was staring at me from heavy lidded eyes. It was the look I had come to know meant "do as you are told or else."

I pushed my plate away and began to slide off of my chair.

“Stay right where you are,” commanded daddy. “You will stay at the table and you will eat what is on your plate.”

I sat down and stared at the plate before me. There were chunks of tender meat and slices of celery covered with a light, fluffy sauce. It smelled delicious but I knew I wouldn’t like it. I refused to taste it.

Momma and daddy proceeded to eat, forks going up and down delivering savory morsels to their waiting lips. Momma speared a piece of bread on her fork and soaked up the remaining sauce on her plate. She held out the fork to me and begged me to try it. I was steadfast in my refusal.

Dinner was finally over and momma began clearing the table. Daddy stood up, lit a cigarette in anticipation of relaxing in the living room as he read the paper. He walked out of the kitchen and I followed in hasty retreat.

“Where do you think you’re going?” boomed daddy.

“To play,” I informed him.

“Not before you finish your dinner,” directed daddy in a firm voice, with eyes staring right into mine. “After dinner you play,” he said as he sauntered into the living room to his favorite chair by the window.

I stood on the threshold, teetering back and forth as I deliberated what I was going to do. I waited until daddy was settled in his chair and completely engrossed with the paper before I ventured out into the hallway.

“Stop right there, Stella!” You’re not going anywhere!”

He crossed the living room in four strides and entered the hallway, blocking my exit to anywhere. “Back into the kitchen,” he directed. He took me firmly by the arm and led me back to the kitchen table and plunked me onto my chair at the table. “Finish that and then you can play. If you don’t eat it, then I’ll have to punish you. And your momma” he continued. I thought I saw a sly wink directed towards momma.

I stared at the plate through a torrent of tears. I picked up the fork and poked and prodded the remains of my dinner. I wouldn’t eat but I couldn’t let momma be punished for something I wouldn’t do. Daddy stared at me from his vantage point in the living room. I sat at the lonely kitchen table. My chin trembled as I sobbed. I brushed tears away as they rolled down my cheeks.

Slowly I speared a piece of meat, examined it thoroughly and hesitantly popped it into my mouth. I was determined to swallow without chewing. It was still warm and the pungent smell of spices teased my dormant taste buds.

I swallowed fast and forked another piece into my mouth - and another - and another. The well of tears dried up and my sobs ended as I proceeded to devour the best food I had ever tasted. I broke pieces of bread and soaked up the remaining sauce and pieces of meat. I licked my fingers, relishing each last taste of this divine meal.

“Okay, I’m finished, daddy,” I chirped as I skipped through the living room and towards the stairs leading to my playroom and waiting dolls.

“Did you finish your dinner?” questioned daddy.

“Yep,” I informed him as I continued my way up the have it again next Sunday,” I shouted, as I ran up the stairs.

Daddy shook his head and sighed and returned to the news of the world.

Money was scarce but we never knew it. We felt loved and cherished and with so many friends and daily adventures, we never lacked for something to do or someone to do it with.

Disgusting, aren't we?
Stella (right), about 4 years old!!
Kelly (left), Penny (center)
....enjoying lollipops at the park in Reading, PA

THE TRAIN

Woo-oooo-ooo; woo-oooo-ooo! The shrill sound of the train whistle blasted through the still summer air, disturbing the quiet of an early June day, alerting us to the impending arrival of the train. We stopped the current game of the hour, scattering the ball and multi-colored jacks everywhere. In unison we arose for the adventure which was to come.

Kally, Lula, Mary and I strutted out the backyard gate, giggling and juggling for the place of prominence, leader of the little band of collaborators. I emerged victorious this day and proudly led my friends to the train trestle. We marched in unison, swinging skinny arms in rhythm, sandaled feet keeping a proper cadence.

The train ran daily through the center of town, dividing Reading into "uptown" and "downtown." It would chug its way through the town on a daily schedule, and our game would send us shrieking in fear and delight, covered with particles of coal dust and soot. We loved the ritual and eagerly awaited the arrival of the train every day. The wooden overpass bridged the distance between "uptown" and "downtown", allowing us to observe the train's progress while peeping through the metal grate of the bridge, watching the train as it puffed its way on the tracks far below us.

"Here it comes," I screamed in my capacity of leader for the day. "I see it; I see it!" We stood against the high fence, peering through the spaces of the chain link barricade, waiting for the supreme moment. We lined up, with Lula, Mary and Kally standing impatiently behind me.

"Woo-oooo-ooo; wo-oooo-ooo; chug—-chug—-chug——" the train was coming closer and closer. "Yay, Yay!," we screamed in unison, dropping on our knees to look through the grate at the fast approaching iron monster below us.

Billows of steam snaked their way upwards through the grating, enveloping us in a warm white cloud. We were no longer visible to each other for we were wrapped in our own warm cocoons for the moment. We stood in awed silence waiting for the cloud to slowly disappear and our vision to be restored. "Chug—-chug—-chug—-; wo-oooo-ooo; wo-oooo-ooo."… and then, silence as the train wound its way around the tracks, away from Reading, away from four small ardent admirers, onward to another city.

"Whew," I wheezed, "that was the BEST cloud ever!" and waved the remnants of the steaming billows away from me. "I never saw one that big; never in my whole life!" and Kally, Lula and Mary voiced their unanimous agreement. The very best!

Slowly, the billows disappeared into the atmosphere and there we stood, four youngsters in coal-speckled sundresses, content and happy, wide grins emerging through dusty little faces.

"Okay, whose turn tomorrow?", I yelled, leading the way back to our front stoop and the waiting game of jacks.

PARASOL PARADE ON REED STREET

Mid-July. A quiet hush hovered over Reed Street. It was too hot to conceive of doing anything more vigorous than trying to stay cool. The sun beat down on the concrete sidewalks. It burned the few blades of grass that were still green. Not a wisp of breeze. All was quiet on Reed Street.

Once again, I refused to be confined to my bedroom for the dreaded afternoon nap. I wanted to splash in my wading pool and work on my suntan. In desperation, momma filled the pool. I plunked myself into the tepid water and waited for the suntan process to begin. Every few minutes I made my waterlogged way into the kitchen to ask momma to check my tan lines. Every few minutes, she would exclaim in awe, "My, what a nice tan!" and off I'd waddle, back to my self-made resort.

I sat there, burning but refusing to admit defeat. The iron gate to our back yard creaked open and I glanced up, barely able to see through the sunny haze. Lula and Mary paraded in, wearing identical sundresses and flaunting their latest acquisition. They each had a paper parasol; identical twins, identical sundresses, identical parasols.

I hurled myself up from my watery confines and padded over to where they stood. "Hi, Stella," they said in unison, twirling the parasols into a wild whirl of color. I went straight for Lula and without asking, snatched the parasol from her hands. Her brown eyes widened, the crookedly-cut bangs obscuring her view. Her mouth formed a wide **O**, with a loud wail soon emerging. Her twin and protector, Mary, rushed to her defense, grabbing my wrist in an effort to retrieve her sister's little parasol. With Herculean strength, I seized her parasol with my free hand and now I had two parasols!

I strutted; I twirled; I whirled; I was magnificent! The twins stood there, mirror images of surprise, unable to move. I had possession of their prize parasols and action had to be taken. In an instant, as if propelled by the same force, they came straight at me. The parasols were grabbed from my hands and placed back into the rightful hands of their owners. They now strutted, twirled and whirled. Grinning, they made their way to the gate for the return journey home. I quickly slipped on my red sandals and prepared to give chase. I was not going to give up the little parasols. Lula and Mary sauntered out and walking side by side, whirled the parasols into a flurry of wild colors. I ran, stumbling as I hit a crack in the sidewalk, and came up behind them. Shrieking, I grabbed Lula by the bow of her sundress with my right hand, and snatched Mary with my left. They accelerated their pace and their vocal protests escalated. They sprinted up the street, with me trailing behind, clutching the handfuls of fabric I had snatched, refusing to let go. Their screams, and my howls, brought the entire neighborhood rushing out to see what was causing such pandemonium and disturbing a peaceful afternoon.

The sight of the twins running, dragging me behind them, parasols somehow still twirling in the air, was one never experienced before and never duplicated since. Mothers sat on doorsteps, weak from laughter. Siblings, friends and neighborhood youth formed a cheering section. We ran on and on.

Momma rushed up behind me, snatching me by my bathing suit straps, pulling me loose from the grip I had on the twins. Lula and Mary ran into their mother's waiting arms, finding snug safety in her ample lap. My march back home was a march in defeat. I hung my head in shame; tears ran down my face, with random hiccups interrupting the sobs. I once had two parasols and now, not even one.

In desperation, momma wiped my eyes, drying my tears and promised to get a parasol for me. She deposited me back into the safe confines of my wading pool, locking the gate against any other surprise visits. My spirit was deflated; my ego was bruised; my selfishness was unsatisfied.

Momma, in an effort to preserve her sanity and restore peace and quiet to Reed Street again, went in search of a parasol. She

Lula (left), Mary (right)

he twins maneuvered her way down to the basement, rummaging through discarded items in search of a miracle. Soon, she found a battered and broken umbrella and dislodged it from a pile of odds and ends. It was red, it was big, it was perfect. Momma straightened the bent and broken frame. She pinned the fabric where it had torn loose and tied a big red bow to the curved wooden handle. "Here, Stella," she said. "Here's your very special parasol." I looked at it, scrutinizing every inch. A smile soon creased my suntanned, tear-streaked face. This was indeed a very special parasol. I gave momma my best grin, and kissed her.

All afternoon, I paraded around and around within the confines of my back yard. Four yards up the street, I could see two pairs of identical brown eyes staring at me. "Hi, Lula; hi, Mary," I shouted. "Look at

MY parasol," I taunted, twirling it into a red frenzy. My umbrella was better than theirs!

My mother channeled her creative talents into sewing clothes for herself and for me. I always had new dresses, made from left-over remnants bought at discount from the textile factory. Dresses did not impress me as I had so many, but new shoes and new hats brought ecstasy to my young life.

SHOES AND HATS

I didn't really care much about new dresses. Momma was always making me clothes, so a new dress hanging in my closet was not a major event in my estimation.

Shoes, however, were special. I loved going to the shoe store with momma to pick out new Easter shoes, summer sandals or school shoes. I would climb up the little stool and step up onto the platform of the x-ray machine. I would place my feet squarely in the designated spot and wait for the salesman to press the button. I would lean forward and put my face close to the viewer. There in full view were my feet - not the flesh of them, but the bony skeleton of them. This is how shoe sizes were measured then and I was mesmerized as I looked at the bony images in the viewer. I couldn't figure out what the machine had done to the fleshy part of my feet but I was delighted to look at my bones and count the ten toes, just to be sure.

I would skip home happily, carrying the box with my new shoes, anticipating the first time I would wear them. I would place the box with the new shoes under my bed when I went to sleep, knowing they would be there in the morning and I could wear the new shoes for the first time. No matter that there would be a new dress to go with the new shoes, the shoes were all that mattered!

****

Hats were slowly becoming a part of my wardrobe. I had wool caps for snowy days; a white bunny fur hat to go with my white bunny fur coat and a straw hat to shield me from the sun. My favorite, however, was the navy blue hat with the wide grosgrain ribbon band and streamers. I called them my wings and I loved to run down the street, streamers flapping wildly in the generated breeze. Momma said I would go so fast and so hard that my feet would hit my fanny as I ran. I would turn and ask, "Am I flying, momma? Am I flying?"

"Yes, yes," she would answer as she gently smiled. For there I was, running wild and carefree, fleet of foot and almost airborne by the flapping streamers of my navy blue hat.

Life was so simple then in Reading, PA. Neighbors gathered on front porches every evening. Catching lightning bugs kept the children occupied as parents caught up with the news of the neighborhood. My father had a car - a big gray Oldsmobile - the only one on the block and his offers for rides were never turned down by anyone.

PAGODA

Lightning bugs blinked their way through the darkness, restless birds chirped as they settled in their nests, and stars flickered through the evening haze. Another sweltering summer evening with no relief in sight. The population of Reed Street began to emerge from the inferno of their homes. Children ran helter-skelter, parents greeted other parents. It was Saturday night and chores were done. It was time to seek companions, comfort and conversation.

Momma sat on the front steps, wiping perspiration from her face. She greeted her friends as they, too, settled to watch the evening go by. I squirmed onto the step below her, trying to catch my breath after a hectic game of chase. It was too hot to run, it was too hot to sleep; it was just too hot! Daddy finally emerged from the house, having finished his evening coffee. He stood at the bottom of the steps and lit a cigarette. I watched the smoke spiral upwards, wondering where it went when it reached the sky. The tip of the cigarette alternately glowed and dimmed as daddy took deep puffs. All was quiet.

Suddenly, Lula came running down the street, ending with a screeching halt in front of our house. She was alone, without Mary, her twin. This was most unusual as they always traveled as a pair; double-trouble, they were called. She plopped herself next to me on the bottom step, pushing me towards the edge. I pushed back. She pushed again and I fell onto the concrete pavement. Startled, I began to cry, but before it could escalate, momma scooped me up in her arms and placed me on her lap. I put my head on her chest, my hands covering my eyes, peeping through my fingers to see if momma would send Lula home.

"Lula, where's Mary?," momma asked. "She's sick," Lula announced; "a cold in the nose, she further explained. "I don't have anything to do at home. Can I stay for a little bit?"

Momma patted her on top of her head. Momma was her godmother and momma loved Lula. If momma was her godmother, did that make her my godsister, I pondered. I had no sisters, but the prospect of Lula filling that role did not please me. I relished my role as only child. This I had to think about.

Momma told Lula she could stay, but it was too hot to run around. We could just sit still for a while and cool off. Momma glanced at daddy, silently whispering, "Do something!"

Daddy suddenly flicked the last of his cigarette into the street and announced, "We're all going to the Pagoda! Let's go!"

Momma went scurrying into the house to comb her hair and to gather some fruit and cheese to take on this unexpected excursion. She threw everything into a small basket, covered it with napkins, locked the door, and descended the stairs to the waiting car.

Daddy eased the car away from the sidewalk. Lula waved from the window on one side and I waved from the other. We were going to the Pagoda! We were escaping from the mundane world below and traveling up, up, up to Mt. Penn, where the Pagoda stood, visible to all of Reading below.

The car chugged up the incline, the lights of the Pagoda quietly beckoning and guiding us. Daddy brought the car to a slow stop and parked by the parapet wall . Lula and I jumped out, scrambling in great haste to the stone wall, as Momma ran after us, fearing the worst. She grabbed us before we could scramble up the steps leading to the stone cap where tourists would often sit, dangling their legs over the side, breathing in the pine scented air, and relishing the sights of distant Reading below

Momma warned us to stay close to her, otherwise we would have to return home. Lula and I stared at each other and nodded our heads simultaneously. We walked towards the Pagoda. We gazed at the red and yellow tiles, the red sloping roof and the golden dragons decorating the doors. This was a magic place! "Can we move here, daddy?," I asked. "Nobody lives here, why can't we? You have lots of money!"

Daddy laughed and lit up another cigarette. Momma smiled as she pulled out the fruit and cheese, doling out small samples on the paper napkins for us. "What is this place, anyway?", I asked. Daddy knew everything; he'd tell us. "Yeah, yeah," echoed Lula.

"Well," daddy began slowly, "a very long time ago this was a hotel and people would come and stay. But one day, people stopped coming and the Pagoda is now just a place to visit and enjoy the view."

"Then, why can't you buy it for me?," I demanded. "We need a bigger house, you said; here it is!", I stated, pointing towards the majestic Pagoda, already envisioning myself as the resident princess in her Chinese castle.

"Not for sale," announced daddy; "so, just enjoy visiting, okay?," and with that, he picked up his fruit and cheese, lit another cigarette, and walked over to the stone wall. Momma joined him and beckoned it was safe for us to now come to the wall.

We stood there, gazing over the top of the wall, mesmerized. The stars seemed closer, the moon was so much larger, and it definitely was cooler up here. Truly, this was heaven. Lula and I munched grapes, spit watermelon seeds at each other, devoured apples and cheese, and marveled at our magic place.

Daddy walked over and lifted me up, placing my sandaled feet firmly on the stone cap and held me tightly. "See, Stella; see below? There's our house," he said, pointing vaguely to a distant point. "Oh, yeah," I confirmed; "I see it!"

"My turn, my turn," Lula shouted impatiently. Daddy planted me next to momma and lifted Lula, placing her on the wall. "See? see?," he asked. "What do you see?"

"Eeeeeeee," screamed Lula, "Eeeeeee, I see A——mer——-i——ca; A—-mer——i——ca!"

****

How small and wonderful our world was then.

My favorite fruit (even to this day) was watermelon. My father would carry the melon on his shoulders, into the kitchen and plunk it on the wooden table. Momma would then look for the sharpest knife in the kitchen drawer to carve into this splendid green globe. If it was the first melon of the season, she would make a sign of the cross over the rind with the knife, thanking God for this goodness and then would carefully plunge the knife into the melon. Juices would ooze out onto the table and drip onto the linoleum floor but no one cared. Momma would place the ruby red pieces on a plate and place it in the ice box as close to the huge block of ice as possible so that it would chill in a hurry. I was wild with anticipation.

SUMMER MEMORY

Summertime meant watermelon. Warm afternoons would find me sitting on the back porch steps, usually in my bathing suit (a most appropriate attire) hungrily devouring slices of watermelon. The sweet juices would drip down my face as I slurped the luscious nectar from the rind.

I would spit out the black shiny seeds to see how far they would go. Weeks later tiny green stems and leaves would sprout where seeds had been trampled into the dirt and I would envision my very own watermelon patch.

If asked, I would tell you my favorite supper on a hot summer night would be watermelon, feta cheese and bread. No matter what momma had cooked, if there was watermelon in the ice box, that was what I ate, despite momma's warnings to taste what she had prepared.

Every morning, Mrs. Pete, our next door neighbor, would watch momma hanging freshly washed sheets out to dry. "Ahhh, good morning, Maria," she would say. "I see Stella had too much watermelon again last night."

And how momma would laugh.

There was no such thing as a baby-sitter back then. Parents would take children with them or one parent would stay home with them or else everyone stayed home. As a result, I was introduced to shopping at an early age, escorting momma to the corner grocery store or the nearby department stores. My shopping skills were in the making at an early age.

READING, PA.'s MOST WANTED

The November sun struggled through the gray clouds. It was cold, but no snow as yet. With my mittened hand held securely by momma, I hopped and skipped beside her. This was my first trip to the new corner grocery store and I anticipated a new adventure.

Momma pushed the heavy glass door open and we hurried inside, the wind pushing us from behind. I helped momma select a cart, one with squeaky, wobbly wheels, and we pushed it down the narrow aisles. Momma stopped before the stacked canned goods, warning me not to dare touch anything. I put my hands behind my back, clutching my fingers together tightly, just to be sure. Cans of soup, peas, corn went flying into the cart as momma and I inched our way down the aisle. The meat counter glistened and momma stopped to ponder her choices. I didn't like what was on display. Red hunks of meat, white mounds of chicken, fish staring blankly into space....what was momma planning to feed us, I wondered.

To my left, I saw the colorful display of vegetables. Bright greens, yellows, reds. Vegetables weren't exactly my favorite but they were prettier to look at than the butcher's display. I shook free of momma's hand and approached the produce. I touched the green peppers, squeezed the tomatoes. I picked dry onion skins off of an onion that had escaped the bin and was now rolling around on the floor. How crunchy, crackly the onion skins were. I liked the way they slithered off of the onion and stayed in my hand. I put a few into my purse, the little patent leather one which matched my new shoes, and I continued on down the aisle. My fingers trailed over every vegetable. I liked the broccoli "trees," the mounds of lumpy cauliflower "snowballs" and, best of all, the shiny, purple eggplants.

At the end of the vegetable counter, I turned the corner and headed for the fruit display. I knew momma would buy lots of fruit and I decided to inspect the variety of offerings. I glimpsed momma traveling at high speed toward me, the cart squealing, its wheels going in every direction but forward. I waved to her, signaling that I was behaving and pointed in the general direction of my next stop.

Huge wooden crates were stacked high, filled with red, glistening "marbles." I had never seen anything like this. My curiosity propelled me closer. I touched the box and put my hand on top of the "marbles," mixing them in a big circle. They were so small. They rolled between my fingers. The color was a deep, deep red, just like the wine momma would serve whenever we had company. The overhead lights glistened on the water droplets covering this new discovery. What were these little red "marbles?" Were they to eat? To play with? For decoration? I had to know.

Cautiously looking to my left and right, I revolved slowly, making certain no one was in sight anywhere. I reached out and I took one. I took one "marble" for my very own. Quickly, I unsnapped my purse and dropped my latest find into it and the "marble" settled snugly among the yellow onion skins.

Momma was ready to leave. We made our quick way home, momma to cook and I to show daddy my new treasure. I slammed the front door closed and threw my coat on the nearest chair, running into the living room. Daddy was sitting in his favorite chair reading the paper by the last remnants of the November daylight streaming through the sheer curtains. I stood in front of him, waiting for him to glance up from his reading. I shifted from one foot to the other.

Waiting no longer, I jumped onto his lap, clinging to his arm to keep from sliding off. He put the paper down and took off his glasses, rubbing his eyes. Although I had intruded into his few moments of solitude, he did not turn me away. "Well," he asked, "did you buy me anything good for dinner?"

I giggled….that was momma's job! I wiggled into a more comfortable spot on his lap, ready to share my new-found treasure. "Wait and see what I have!", I whispered, digging through the contents of my purse, which now consisted of three nickels, a handkerchief, old chewing gum saved for future use, the crinkly onion skins and the shiny red "marble." I pinched the "marble" between my fingers and held it out proudly for inspection, allowing my daddy to share this most recent find. "Look!", and I pushed the "marble" closer for him to see.

"Do you know what this is?", he asked. I shrugged my shoulders.

"It's a cranberry," he informed me. "Where did you get it?"

"At the store….from the box; momma took me to the store," I answered, feeling slightly uncomfortable now. This was not going well.

Daddy stood up, abruptly landing me on the floor. He pulled me up by the hand and grabbed my coat as we passed the chair by the door, telling me to put it on….fast.

"Maria," he yelled to momma, "We're going out. Stella has something to return to the store, and a confession to make."

"Who cares," I thought; I would never eat cranberries anyway!"

CRIME AND PUNISHMENT

Holding momma's hand as she had taught me, I walked quickly beside her. We were on our way to Pomeroy's Department Store. Momma pushed our way through the revolving door and hurried to the pattern counter. Momma was going to make me a new dress and I had to look at all the choices that were displayed.

I soon became bored as momma pored over the many pattern books. I slid off the stool and told her I would not go far. I wandered up and down the aisles, looking but not touching as I had been warned. All of a sudden, I saw what I had always wanted —- taps for my shoes. I snatched two shiny taps and quickly went back to the safety of my mother's presence. I placed the taps equi-distant on the floor and slowly stomped my left foot on one and my right foot on the other. I twisted my feet with as much strength as I could muster, forcing the little prongs on the taps to take firm hold onto the bottom of my black patent leather Mary Janes.

Tap…tap…tap tap tap…tap…tap…tap tap …..I envisioned myself as another Shirley Temple. I spun around, twirling my pleated skirt, tapping away. Momma looked up from her absorption in the fashion book to locate the source of the distracting, disturbing noise. There I was, tapping, right foot over left foot, back and forth, back and forth. She jumped up, knocking over the stool, quickly grabbed me and hauled me behind the pattern counter.

"What are you doing?" she hissed. "What do you have there?" I held up my foot, almost losing my balance, and displayed the glittering, and by now slightly battered, tap.

"See," I said, "Just like Shirley Temple!" and I put my foot down and proceeded to present her with my repertoire…tap…tap…tap tap tap…tap…tap…In mid-step, I was suddenly propelled forward, momma pulling me by the arm, heading for the manager's office. I was soon face to face with an authority higher than momma, the store manager. I trembled. What to do now? Momma, I could handle, but this was a force I had never envisioned. Momma told the manager of the theft that had just taken place and pointed to my patent leather shoes. "Take them off," she ordered. I looked plaintively at her stern face. I looked at Mr. Manager, who was glowering at me, his eyes piercing right through me. He nodded. Reluctantly, I unbuckled my shoes, first the right, then the left. I gave them to momma. She placed them back in my hands and sternly directed that I remove the taps and give them to the manager. I grimaced. I wiped my teary eyes. I pleaded silently with my saddest, most forlorn expression. All in vain.

"Take them off!"

I pried the little taps off, scratching my fingers in the process and cradled them in the palm of my hand. I looked longingly at them, my dreams of stardom thwarted in their prime. I placed them in Mr. Manager's outstretched hand.

"Thank you," he said. He turned to momma and said, "I hope this will never happen again." I thought I saw a smile flickering in the corner of his stern mouth, but that couldn't be for this was very serious business.

"Thank you for pardoning my daughter; thank you. She turned to me and asked if I had anything to say.

"Yes," I screamed. "I'll NEVER shop at Pomeroy's again!" and I stomped off towards the exit door.

Mr. Manager and momma quickly caught up with me. I stared at Mr. Manager and again said, "Never!".

Momma and Mr. Manager exchanged smiles as I angrily pushed my way back out, never to step foot in Pomeroy's again.

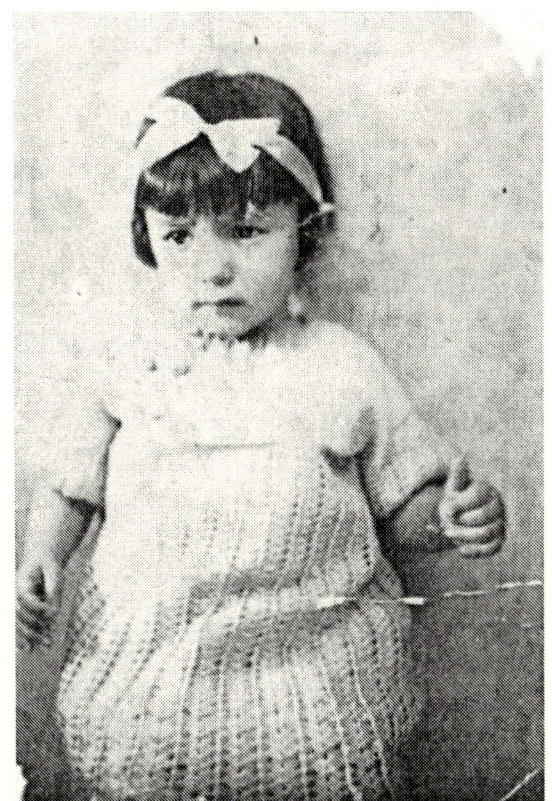

Stella

With the fathers expected to work many long hours to provide for the family, mothers were expected to handle any and all household crises. Case in point:

A MOVING STORY

The movers had just finished depositing the last of the furniture and packing boxes. We had just moved into a bigger house. Momma was running upstairs and back downstairs, creating order out of the chaos. Daddy had gone to work to get away from what he considered a woman's job and I was left to my own devices.

I curled onto the blue velvet sofa and carved a place for myself among the plush cushions. I was sad for I had to leave the only home I had known. Getting used to a new house was an adventure I was hesitant to experience.

I sat, sullen and forlorn, oblivious to all the activity around me. Electricians arrived as painters departed. Furnace repairmen came as well as carpenters. Momma was everywhere, instructing and supervising the ongoing commotion as I watched in bewilderment.

A noise in the far corner startled me. I looked around and saw that I was alone, momma having gone on to other areas of concern. The buzzing noise continued and I inched closer to the source of the noise. There was a small hole in the floor at the far end of the room. I stooped down to get a better look. Suddenly, a thin, black wiggly form emerged slowly from the hole, inching up and up and up towards me.

"A snake, a snake," I screamed as I tried to find my way out through the maze of furniture and boxes. The buzzing continued and the snake kept coming upward and outwards from the hole.

I flung the front door open and ran wildly into the street, screaming "A snake, a snake; there's a snake in my house."

A dog, a mongrel of unknown species, startled by my screams, came running towards me from a yard several doors down. He was soon nipping at my heels as I ran in circles. The dog was yipping and yapping while I was screaming and the snake was unfurling in the living room.

I ran back into the house, mongrel dog still chasing me. My screams ascended to a high crescendo, echoing through the rooms. Momma hurtled down the stairs to my rescue.

"What's happening? What's wrong?" she asked as she faced the fiasco before her. The dog was chasing me, I was chasing it and we had nowhere to go. Momma diverted the dog towards the door and quickly but gently booted it out of the house and back onto the sidewalk. She caught me on my last lap around the living room and pulled me onto the nearby sofa. She brushed my hair out of my eyes and patted my back until my breath settled down to a normal rate. "What happened? Tell me."

"There's a snake in the house! A long, black snake over there," and I pointed to the corner. The snake was coiled, no longer wiggling its way upwards. Momma walked towards the snake, ready to do all she could to protect her only child.

She prodded it with her foot as I wailed in renewed fear. She kicked it and even bent down to touch it as I envisioned momma being devoured by a snake. "No, no, momma, don't touch it!" I screamed in warning.

Suddenly momma sat on the floor as laughter engulfed her. She rocked back and forth in great glee. I stopped wailing and watched momma and wondered if she had gone completely mad.

She pulled the snake from the hole and wound it around her hand. I was speechless. Momma was so brave, I thought. She kept pulling the snake as she came towards me. "Here, here's the snake" she said as she kept winding the black slithery thing around her wrist.

I inched closer for a better look, feeling somewhat safer now. The snake was so skinny and not moving at all. Had momma killed it, I wondered.

“Stella, you silly thing. It’s not a snake. It’s the wire for the radio set we are putting in that corner. The man downstairs was putting the wire through the hole he had drilled. No snake, just wiring for the radio,” she repeated.

I went silently back to my spot on the blue velvet sofa to find comfort and hide my shame.

I was a child with imagination, but often borrowed ideas from others.

OPEN, SESAME.....

THUD! THUD!

The door rattled with the sheer force hurled upon its wooden panels. THUD! THUD!

Once more - THUD! I stopped kicking to rub my sore toe, but soon began the rhythm again. THUD! THUD! I was getting good at this, I thought. Little chips of white paint fluttered down to the concrete steps with each impact. THUD! THUD!

Reed Street was quiet. My friends were taking afternoon naps. No one was running around, playing the games that were part of our daily routine. Momma was in the kitchen cleaning and chopping vegetables for salad. Daddy was sleeping, having just come home from working the night shift. For me, it seemed this was the opportune time to practice a new way of opening the door. I had watched Lillian, an older girl who lived across the street, getting the door to her house open in this new and exciting way. I wanted to test it out myself. It was certainly impressive, I thought. I tried to mimic her rhythm of thuds, but somehow I felt mine were better.

THUD! THUD! THUD!

The door suddenly swung open. I was pulled inside by a centrifugal force. There loomed my daddy in rumpled pajamas, eyes groggy with sleep, his hair standing in tangled wisps.

“What’s going on out here?”, he bellowed. I started to run towards the kitchen and to safety behind momma’s back, but he was too quick for me.

“But…but….but I was only doing what Lillian did,” I said in my self-defense.

"Kicking doors is not what a daughter of mine does. I don't care who you are imitating!", he roared. I had no other self-defense.

Momma stood in the kitchen doorway watching the drama unfold, not coming to my rescue, for daddy was definitely in charge. I blinked back tears, looking up at daddy with a forlorn face. But daddy was like a bear awakened from winter's hibernation. I dared not say more. He gripped my hand in his and walked rapidly towards my room. I was pulled into the room and plopped onto the bed. The soft pink comforter billowed out around me, softening the landing. I heard the door closing, daddy's voice dictating that I was to stay there until I came out with an apology.

I took off my shoes. In my stocking feet, I tiptoed up to the closed bedroom door.

THUD! THUD! THUD!

Hard on the toes, but what an act of defiance.

THUD! THUD! THUD!.......

Summer nights were a magical time. Supper dishes would be washed and put away quickly and the entire neighborhood would emerge from the confines of the row houses to seek conversation and a cool breeze.

SUMMER DELIGHT

I considered myself to be the luckiest girl in the world. Not only did my godfather own an ice cream plant, but my daddy worked on the ice cream wagon. Every summer evening at 7 o'clock, daddy made his rounds through the neighborhood. Every night I had ice cream, any flavor I wanted. Life was very good.

Another hot, sultry summer evening as the neighborhood filled with the usual evening sounds. In order to escape the heat trapped inside the houses, the neighborhood emerged every evening to cool off, to socialize, to relax. Children played, mothers exchanged neighborhood news, fathers discussed the day's events. The sounds of trolley cars, an occasional car horn blast and the far-away toot of a train whistle provided the tempo for the evening. It was our favorite time. The work day had ended, household chores were done, dinnertime had come and gone. It was time to soothe mind and body.

I ran up to momma, my breath coming in short spurts, chest heaving. "What time is it? Is it time yet?" She pulled me down onto the step next to her, wiped my face with her handkerchief and brushed straggly bangs away from my forehead in an effort to cool me down. I had just finished a hectic game of hide and seek and my energy level was in need of refueling. "What time?", I repeated.

Momma looked at her watch which she had carefully placed in her pocket, allowing her wrist freedom from the sweltering confines of the leather band. She showed me the watch. The big hand was on the twelve and the little hand on the seven. It was time for the ice cream wagon.

I ran wildly back to my cronies proclaiming the news. "Come on, come on," I shouted. We plopped down on the curb in a straight and orderly row, wiggling our little bottoms into the most comfortable spot on the hard concrete, clutching our nickels, silently deciding our choice of dessert.

Clop….clop….clop….Pounding hooves announced the arrival of the ice cream wagon. Clop…clop…clop…..There was Toby, my favorite horse, pulling the white wagon with ***Crystal Ice Cream*** in bright red letters on the side. Daddy waved as he made his way up the street, coming to a halt before the grimy and hungry youngsters lined up on the curbside.

"Okay, kids, what do you want?", he asked, preparing for the frenzy which was to follow.

"Vanilla"…. "Strawberry"…… "Chocolate"…… "Popsicle"….. jumbled sounds, frantic waving of tiny hands and little bodies swarming around the wagon soon frightened Toby. He stomped, he snorted, he turned away from the confusion. Daddy leaned out from the wagon and thumped Toby on his left rear flank. "It's okay; it's okay," he assured him. Toby shook his head from side to side, flecks of saliva flying, mane tossing in the air. I gingerly stepped in front of him and rubbed his nose, cooing his name, coaxing him to settle down. I loved Toby and I knew he loved me. Soon, Toby was his usual gentle self and daddy was ready to take our orders

One by one, ice cream concoctions were created, my daddy constructing frozen wonders much to the delight of his small customers. We happily marched away licking the creamy double scoops, faces traced with chocolate fudge, tee shirts used as napkins, hands sticky with the gooey concoctions. We settled on the curbside again and watched the wagon as it made it way up the street, daddy waving goodbye and Toby's rump wiggling from side to side. The neighborhood was quiet again, the only sound being that of little mouths soaking up the last remnants of ice cream cones.

Evening descended, stars appeared, a breeze brought cool relief from the day's heat. We slowly disappeared into our houses, silent, happy, content with the world in which we lived.

****

I remember saying my prayers every night, asking God to bless momma, daddy, my godfather, the horses and especially Toby!

Not having relatives, my circle of adult visitors was limited to neighbors and friends of my parents. I spent a lot of time with my mother and at times would resent any intrusion on our time together.

THE VISIT

The shrill buzz of the doorbell shattered the stillness of a dreary December afternoon. I dropped the doll I was bathing and ran to be the first to greet what must be a visiting neighbor. Momma soon followed and gently pushed me aside as she unbolted the door. I peeped around momma to see who would be coming to visit today, bringing a fresh batch of homemade cookies and the latest neighborhood news.

I stared at the stranger standing on the doorstep. Momma shrieked and I ran upstairs to my room in frightened haste. I could still hear momma shrieking and I trembled in fear at the intrusion of this stranger. Daddy was at work and it was just momma and me at home and now a stranger was in our midst. I huddled under the bedcovers and waited for the worst.

Minutes passed and I heard nothing. I scrambled out from under the covers and tiptoed to the bedroom door. I pulled the door open and looked up and down the empty hallway. I crawled to the stairs and peeped through the railings. There, in the living room, sat my mother and the stranger. I couldn't believe momma had invited this person into our house. She constantly cautioned me not to talk to strangers and there she was sitting next to one.

He sat next to momma, stroking her hand while he talked. Momma leaned over and kissed him on the cheek. I sat frozen on the top step as I watched the two of them. What would I tell daddy?

I ran back into my room to the safety of my bed and the darkness under the covers. I was hungry but I would not venture out. I was cold but would not ask momma for a sweater. I was afraid and knew not what to do. I huddled even deeper under the covers.

"Stella, Stella, where are you?" momma asked as she patted the mountain of blankets and comforter. "What are you doing there?

Come out."

"No; I'm 'fraid."

"Of what?" she asked.

"That scary man in the house," I stammered, eyes wide in fear. I clutched the covers even closer to my trembling body and hid further under their comforting warmth.

Momma started out of my room towards the stairs. "No, no, stay here. The bad man is downstairs."

She turned back and stood by my bed. She started to laugh. I peeped from under the blankets, not believing she could laugh in the midst of danger.

"Oh, Stella, there's no bad man here. That's my cousin, my cousin Jim from Savannah. You'll call him Uncle Jim. He surprised us for a visit. Come down and say hello."

I stayed in my room. My stomach growled with hunger. My throat was parched from thirst, but I would not go downstairs. Momma pleaded and cajoled. I would not budge.

"Fine," momma huffed. "Stay in your room. When your father comes home, you will come downstairs."

The afternoon passed as momma stayed downstairs with the stranger and I remained a prisoner in my room. My curiosity was huge but fear loomed even larger.

I heard the front door slam as daddy announced his arrival. I felt my fear ebbing, knowing that daddy was home. He would chase the stranger away. I heard daddy's voice raised in surprise and the gentle murmur of momma's voice. I detected no fear, no anger, no terror.

By now, hunger was gnawing holes in my stomach. I had not eaten since breakfast and the rumblings and grumblings of my stomach grew louder and louder. I walked to the head of the staircase to see what was happening downstairs. I peered through the banister railings from my favorite vantage point on the top step.

Daddy and momma were sitting on the sofa. The intruder was sitting in daddy's favorite chair across from them. He was sitting in daddy's chair! I couldn't believe it. No one ever sat in daddy's chair. Something was terribly wrong.

I put one foot forward and then the other and crept slowly down the winding staircase. I stopped at the bottom landing and stared into the living room. The brightly lit lamps filled the room with a warm glow. The fireplace was blazing, which was most unusual. This was done only when we had company - very special company. Daddy and the stranger were sipping coffee from the small cups momma used on special occasions. Momma just sat there, munching on a cookie, content and happy.

My curiosity could not be contained. I stood in the hallway at the living room archway, hoping to attract their attention. They kept sipping, munching and talking. I shifted from one foot to the other and the creak of the floorboards finally alerted them to my presence.

Momma looked over and saw me standing in the doorway. She hadn't seen me since early that day but showed no reaction to the fact that I had all but disappeared for those many hours.

"Come in, come in," she said. "This is your Uncle Jim from Savannah. Say hello." She motioned for me to come in but I stood frozen to the spot. My gaze skipped from daddy, to momma, to the stranger. I directed a feeble smile towards daddy and momma. I glared at the stranger as he waved at me.

Momma walked over to where I stood. She grasped my hand firmly in hers and began to lead me into the living room. "Say hello to Uncle Jim," she instructed. "He's going to stay with us for a few days. Say hello."

I bolted out of the room, up the stairs, into my room and under the covers. I waited. And I waited. By now, I was starving but I was not joining the happy group downstairs. I would stay in my room and waste away to nothingness.

I snuggled under the covers and whimpered. I was so very hungry and momma didn't seem to care. She was too busy with her cousin. I hated him for coming to our house and disrupting our routine. I heard the door to my room open. I lifted a corner of the blanket and gazed at daddy as he came towards me. He was balancing a tray of food with one hand and carried a pitcher of milk with the other. I popped out from my hiding place and sat on the edge of the bed, legs swinging wildly back and forth. "Here, Stella. I brought you some food. You have to eat."

I eyed the morsels before me and quickly picked up the scrambled egg sandwich. Scrambled eggs with pieces of asparagus throughout, spread evenly on white bread; my favorite sandwich. I gobbled the sandwich in huge bites, licking every morsel off of the plate. A tangerine was next, followed by a piece of apple pie and a glass of milk. Daddy watched as I ate. He wiped my face with a napkin and asked if I wanted to go back downstairs with him. I shook my head from side to side. "No!"

Next morning, momma came into my room to help me get dressed for the day. She helped me into my underwear and clothes. She slipped shoes and socks on my feet. She kissed my face as she brushed my hair. "Now," she said, "let's go down for breakfast. Daddy and Uncle Jim are waiting."

I dove under the covers and refused to budge. After many minutes of pleading, momma slammed the bedroom door shut and stomped downstairs. A little later daddy came in with hot cocoa and toast and kept me company while I enjoyed breakfast in bed.

Lunch and dinner followed. For two days, daddy served me three meals a day as momma totally ignored me. I didn't care.

On the third morning after the usual cocoa and toast, daddy told me I was not being polite. Uncle Jim had come a long way to see us and would be leaving the next day. Daddy dressed me, took me in his arms and made his way down the winding stairs to the kitchen.

Uncle Jim and momma were sitting at the kitchen table. They smiled and gasped in surprise at my appearance. Uncle Jim smiled, his mustache stretching across his face, and said he was happy to see me. I looked at daddy for assurance. Daddy said it was all right to say hello, for this was not a stranger, but a relative.

I bent forward from daddy's arms and tentatively touched Uncle Jim's hand as I mumbled a greeting. I jumped down from daddy's arms and dashed into the dining room and staked claim under the large dining room table. There I stayed for the rest of the day.

Later that evening, Uncle Jim came into the room. I kept quiet, watching his every move. "I wonder where Stella is?" he muttered. "I have a very special present for Stella, but I can't find her." He walked around the room, pausing near me, his black-shoed feet almost touching me and still I wouldn't move.

"Well," I heard him say, "I guess Stella has gone away. I'll just have to leave this for her." I saw him bend down and place a big box by one of the table legs. I heard him walk away and out of the room. I crawled towards the box and ripped the ribbon and big bow away. I pulled the top off and threw the many layers of tissue helter-skelter about the room. I reached in and pulled out a teddy bear. It was a cuddly, brown teddy bear, the softest, warmest, biggest teddy bear I had ever seen.

My eyes grew wide in wonderment as I gazed at this teddy bear. I hugged the teddy bear close to my fluttering heart and kissed its friendly face. The room was quiet and I knew no one was in the dining room. I squirmed out from my hiding place, dragging the bear behind me. Voices drifted towards me in a low hum and I followed the sound to the living room doorway. Momma and daddy sat on the sofa and Uncle Jim relaxed on daddy's chair by the window. They looked happy and totally unconcerned about my whereabouts.

I looked into the room. The crystal chandelier caught the glow of the logs in the fireplace and showered the room with rainbows. The crackling and hissing of the logs, the dancing shower of rainbow drops and the low murmur of voices lured me within. I shuffled over to momma and squeezed between her and daddy, placing the teddy bear proudly on my lap. I glowed.

"Where did you get that?" momma asked.

Daddy leaned over and patted the bear. "What is its name?" he asked.

Uncle Jim just smiled. His mustache arched over his mouth and his brown eyes twinkled. I studied him closely and decided that he was not a bad man after all.

I jumped off of the sofa and ran over to Uncle Jim. I kissed him quickly and mumbled, "I love you."

And I ran to my room, hugging my new teddy bear, to the waiting warm cocoon of my bed.

No fancy toys, no playgrounds, no camps and sports - imagination was our game!

THE ICE AGE

A huge block of ice slithered down the chute, bouncing to its final destination, emerging through the hinged metal door and coming to a stop at the edge of the concrete threshold. The customer entitled to this chunk of coolness presented a ticket, lifted the icy mass and quickly departed for home.

We peeked from around the corner, tripping over each other, pushing and shoving to get a better view. Kally stepped forward, ran across the street and plopped down on the bottom step in front of her house. Living across the street from the ice house was a stroke of luck for us, for she was the sentry, the lookout for us. She would sit innocently on the front steps, her eyes darting from side to side, ever vigilant.

She gave us the signal. All was clear. We cautiously came out from our hiding place. We stood in front of the metal door, counting the ice shards lying on the concrete sill, anticipating the chunks waiting for us on the other side of the metal door. Mary scooped the now melting ice shards into her hands and made her way across the street to join Kally. Lula and I joined energies, forcing the hinged metal door open and peered inside. A blast of chill air hit us, sending us sprawling backwards. We peeked again and with eyes slowly adjusting to the dark recesses, we saw the sparkling array of ice, tiny icebergs waiting for us. Lula scooped up the first handful. I held up the hem of my dress to form a receptacle for the ice and she began to deposit the day's loot into the billowing material. We had several knife-sharp shards and five large chunks. More than enough to quench the thirst of four youngsters. Lula and I staggered across the street holding onto my water-soaked skirt and deposited the day's catch on the porch. We grabbed our share of the frozen treasure and made our way to the sidewalk curb. We plopped down in an orderly row, noisily sucking on the pilfered ice.

Neighbors were our extended family and we youngsters, in turn, provided them with their entertainment.

MR. PETE

My favorite place in our small backyard was by the fence. It wasn't very high, but being only four years old, I couldn't quite see over the top yet. Momma had planted pretty flowers along the border and I liked to squish my toes in the soft dirt. I would peek through the slats on a regular basis, just to be sure nothing more exciting was going on in Mr. Pete's yard.

Mr. Pete was a kind man. He told me funny stores. He gave me hard candy to stuff into my pockets. He didn't tell momma when I poured my glass of milk down the drain. And, best of all, he had a son I wanted to marry when I grew up.

Mr. Pete was my friend. He protected me from the likes of Lula and Mary, who lived down the street. They teased me and made me cry. "Be careful, Stella," he would say, "Lula and Mary are in their yard." I would turn and look down the length of four yards, spotting Lula and Mary in their identical outfits. I would wave and go back to my dolls, dressing them and stuffing them in and out of the new babydoll carriage I had recently acquired. I was oblivious to anything but the care of "my babies." I covered them and cradled them and pushed them back and forth in the carriage. I had so many responsibilities with these babies.

One day, Mr. Pete announced, "Lula and Mary just said you were ugly!"

I stood up, dropping the carriage blanket in my haste and looked him straight in the eye as best I could from my limited height. Again, Mr. Pete reminded me that Lula and Mary were taunting me. I stormed over to the other side of the fenced-in yard where I could get a better view of the twins. I placed my hands on my hips and in my loudest voice, screamed: "I am NOT ugly. I'm little, and I'm cute, and my daddy is big and rich and fat and he'll beat you all up"! With that, I trotted a hasty retreat back to my dolls.

Mr. Pete just stood there, grinning, enjoying the fracas he had created. Lula and Mary responded, screaming, "You are, too!"

Again, I ran to the fence and waving a fist, I again verified my daddy's merits. Mr. Pete called me over and patted me on the head and told me not to worry, for the twins were just teasing me. I looked up at him for assurance, a guarantee of safety. "Come here," he said. I walked over to the fence, assured that the best part of knowing Mr. Pete was to come. He put his hands on my shoulders, lifting me slightly off the ground and swung me back and forth, back and forth and lifted me over the fence to visit with Mrs. Pete and their son, the man I wanted to marry.

Being an only child had its merits, but at times I longed for a brother or sister - someone to "fight with" was my compelling reason.

GUESS WHO'S COMING TO DINNER?

It was a Saturday afternoon. I was confined to the house getting over the last stages of a bad cold. I was very bored. Momma had played games with me, let me adorn myself with her clothes, provided coloring books and crayons and even read me a story. But I was tired of the familiar.

"What can I do?" I whined, tugging at momma's apron. "What can I do? I have nothing to do!" I followed momma around the kitchen. Momma was reaching her limit of tolerance. I could tell from the brilliance of her eyes. I watched as she quickly walked over to the phone.

"Hello, Rose? Maria here. Can Kally come over and play with Stella for a little while?" A pause. "Yes, she's better; much better, but I don't want her outside for another day or two.Okay, that's fine," she commented as she replaced the received. "Stella," momma began, "Kally is coming over to play for a while. Be good and play nice."

Kally was soon knocking at the kitchen door and in she came, rosy cheeks and sparkly eyes, coal black hair flying every which way.

"I'm here; so, let's play," she announced. I led her to my playroom and we sat on the linoleum-covered floor as I displayed my many toys. I gave her first choice and a game of jacks commenced. The slick linoleum floor made scooping up the jacks much easier, allowing each of us to tie for first place more often than not. Paper dolls were brought out next. We cut out new dresses for the dolls and acted out little plays, creating dialogue as we went along. Soon tiring of sitting on the floor, we jumped up simultaneously and began throwing a small rubber ball back and forth, back and forth, only to finally tumble back down on the floor in a vain attempt to catch the ball as it slid under the wooden cedar chest and rolled to the furthermost corner.

I could sense Kally was getting bored. Kally wanted to go home. She had a big house with many sisters and it was always filled with friends and laughter. Kally wanted to go home and be part of the dynamic household. Despite all the noise I generated, our house was quiet and mild by comparison. Kally started packing up the toys and putting the paper dolls in their proper boxes.

"Don't you want to stay and eat with me?" I asked. Kally shook her head. "Don't you want to listen to the radio stories?"

Nope," said Kally, and she started to get up from the floor.

"Let's take our socks off and run on the linoleum," I offered. We loved the squeaky noises our toes would make as we ran around the room on the shiny linoleum. Again, Kally refused.

"What's for supper?" I yelled down to momma. Maybe momma's evening meal would be just the enticement Kally needed.

"Stew," momma answered, "with lots of potatoes……and we'll have ice cream for dessert. Does Kally want to stay?"she asked. Kally shook her head frantically, her hair flinging, swinging from side to side, her eyes wide in a panic mode. It was very clear she wanted to go home.

"Momma, guess who's gonna stay for dinner!," I announced. "Kally!"

For there I was, sitting on Kally as she sprawled prone on the linoleum floor. I had flattened her out on the cold floor, squatted my skinny body on Kally's stomach and held her hostage.

"Momma, did you hear? Kally's gonna stay for dinner!"

Entertaining me every waking hour was a constant challenge for my mother. Often exhausted, she would give in to my requests, usually ending up with dire results.

IF THE SHOE FITS, WEAR IT!

“In the name of all that’s holy, Stella, be quiet!”, screamed momma in total exasperation. She had had an exhausting morning and was eager to rest her weary body until it was time to start preparations for dinner. Thirty minutes was all she wanted.

Momma pulled all the shades down, darkening the house and cooling it off somewhat. She kicked off her shoes and settled back on the living room couch. She closed her eyes, inviting sleep to come. I watched her. I watched her eyelids flutter. I watched her face relax. I watched her clenched hands slowly unfold. Momma slept.

What was I supposed to do? The doors were locked, shades were drawn and I had nothing to do. A nap was out of the question. I had to find something to entertain me. I tiptoed out of the living room and roamed from room to room. It was quiet everywhere. The clock ticked, the refrigerator shuddered on and off and I continued to roam. Nothing to do.

I walked into momma and daddy’s bedroom and stood in front of the big triple mirror. I looked steadfastly at my image. I made faces; I twirled; I twisted from side to side, looking at the many images bouncing back from the three-sided mirror. I opened the closet door. I found momma’s new shoes. Blue leather sling-back high heels. I sat down on the floor and proceeded to insert my sweaty, dirty bare feet into momma’s shoes. I held onto the closet door and stood up, tottering unsteadily, a clear two inches taller than I had been just seconds ago. This was exhilarating. I clomped slowly over to the bed, ankles bending, knees shaking. This was wonderful!

I made a slow, unsteady return to the living room, hands gripping the wall with every step. I shuffled over to momma but she was still sleeping. I leaned over closer and whispered, “Momma; momma; are you sleeping?” No answer. I slowly lifted one eyelid and peered in. I lifted the other eyelid. “Momma?”

She sat up abruptly, glancing about, trying to assess her whereabouts, still lost in sleep. “What’s wrong? What happened?”, she asked.

“Nothing, momma. I want to play with your shoes.” She sighed and with great restraint reminded me that wearing high heels was not allowed. She would not let me and daddy definitely prohibited it.

“But momma, I walked all the way over here,” I whined. I proceeded to strut from one end of the living room to the other. I fell once, but quickly resumed the pace, perfecting each step. “See, momma!”

“No,” she stated; “No!”

My eyes filled with tears, the whining began, the crying escalated. I pleaded, I begged, I stomped my feet and made every promise on earth just for five minutes with the blue high heels.

In desperation, momma finally agreed but with strong warnings of caution and safety. I assured her I was becoming quite adept at this and not to worry. I gently pushed her back onto the couch for the remainder of her nap. I tested the kitchen door. Through some oversight, it had been left unlocked. I carefully and quietly made my way out to the walkway in the backyard. I clomped my way back and forth, up and down, here and there. Momma’s shoes were becoming scuffed and the heels were beginning to wobble but my journey continued. I imagined myself as a model, as a movie star, as a working girl. It was glorious! I rejoiced in my excursion around the perimeter of the yard.

A car pulled up into the driveway. The door slammed. I heard daddy roar, “What do you think you are doing?” I was scared. I was really in for it now! Daddy had absolutely refused permission to ever wear momma’s shoes. It was too dangerous, he had said.

“Hah,” I thought, “if he could only see me navigate this sidewalk!” I smiled and tottered forth towards him on the high heels. “Momma said I could,” I proclaimed, quite smug with my achievement.

With that, he lifted me by the arms, shaking the shoes off my little feet, dropping them onto the grass below and proceeded to carry me inside.

"Maria....Maria!" He was furious, I could tell, and I refrained from wiggling. I rationalized the situation. If momma had said it was okay, how could it be so wrong?

It was very wrong. Daddy fussed at momma, citing the dangers of letting me stomp around in high heels. He showed her the damaged shoes and told her she would just have to make do.

Momma had to explain. I was punished, and daddy remained the final authority.

Visiting was the social outlet for the mothers. Visiting was a special event, requiring dressing up, often walking many blocks to the friend to be visited and sharing several hours of conversation, coffee and cookies. I liked that part, but I hated the......

LADIES IN BLACK

By age four, I knew I did not like old ladies. I had to call them "Yaya." They wore black all the time. They screeched in delight when they saw me and marveled at how much I had grown. They pinched my cheeks and patted my bottom. I had to kiss them and the hairs on their chins scratched my face. Their hair was wisps of white peeking out from under a black headscarf. When they laughed, I noticed missing teeth. They drooled. They scared me.

When they visited I had to wear a dress and help momma serve them coffee. When we visited them, I had to sit very still and show them what a good girl I was. In church, I had to offer them my seat. They always said "yes," which meant I would have to stand by momma or else try to sit still on her lap.

I announced to momma one day how much I did not like the "yayas." She admonished me for my lack of respect. She reminded me that she, too, would one day be an old lady. "What will you do then, Stella, when I am old and gray and they call me 'Yaya'?"

"I'll run away!" I calmly advised her. "Yep, I'll run away."

Fifteen years later, I began my penance. I began taking care of momma right after daddy died and for the next forty years I had my very own little old lady who screeched in delight when she saw me, marveled at how much I had grown, pinched my cheeks and patted my bottom. I kissed her, hugged her and combed the wispy white hair. She didn't scare me.

Visiting also meant "souvenirs" to me. Momma tried to explain.

OL' ROCKING CHAIR GOT ME

Momma finnaly finished bathing me and helped me climb out of the tub. She had rubbed and scrubbed until I glowed. My knees had been scoured with Bon Ami in a final attempt to erase the ground-in dirt that I managed to accumulate daily.

Enveloped in a big, fluffy towel, I shuffled towards my bedroom, bare feet leaving a trail of wet footprints on the hallway carpeting. Momma quickly tossed an undershirt over my head, pulling my arms into the appropriate armholes. A pair of panties and a matching petticoat were quickly placed on my shivering body. I watched momma as she sorted through the clothes hanging in the closet. She pulled wire hangers off of the wooden pole, inspecting and rejecting each item hanging from them. I followed her every move and knew not what was to transpire.

A blue and white sailor dress was the final choice. She pulled it off the hanger and held it up against me. She stretched the dress across my chest and smoothed it down against my legs. "Hmmm," she muttered, "it still fits. Okay, Stella, let's put on the dress. We have to hurry."

The dress was quickly buttoned on, the red sailor tie knotted and the big sailor collar smoothed against my back. White socks and black patent leather Mary Janes were next and I still hadn't a clue of where I was going. Momma stepped back to look at me and smiled at the perfection that stood before her.

She took me by the hand and guided me out of the bedroom and down the stairs to the front entryway. She grabbed her purse, keys and gloves from a nearby table and opened the front door, never letting go of my hand.

Reaching the bottom step, I stopped abruptly and refused to go any further. "Where are you taking me all dressed up? I want to play!" I glowered at her, my thick eyebrows furrowing into one straight line.

"We're going to visit Mrs. Nasis," she informed me. "You like Mrs. Nasis."

Mrs. Nasis! Why were we going there? Mrs. Nasis was the priest's wife. Had I done something so bad that it warranted a visit to the priest's house? I reviewed the past few days and could think of nothing that would justify a visit with Mrs. Nasis.

Momma pulled me along and I walked in silence next to her. I looked up at her and she seemed happy and relaxed. Perhaps my gloom and doom were unfounded. I decided to remain quiet and endure the next hour or so.

We stopped in front of a big house with glistening windows and etched glass in the front door. "We're here," momma informed me. She pushed the white button on the doorframe and I heard a distant buzzing. The door soon opened and there stood Mrs. Nasis. Her white hair was neatly groomed into waves and a big bun in the back. She wore a dark blue dress with a white lace collar. Her dark eyes twinkled as she greeted me first. "Hello, Stella; welcome. Come in with momma and visit, won't you?"

Momma urged me forward and I ventured past the front door into the hallway and followed Mrs. Nasis into the living room. Everything glistened and the aroma of something wonderful baking wafted in from the kitchen. I envisioned a plateful of cookies, which certainly would make the afternoon worthwhile.

The ladies talked as I sat on the armchair by the window. I looked at the birds chirping in the tree and watched squirrels as they chased each other through the tree branches. I leafed through magazines and looked at pictures and wished I could read. I was beginning to get bored.

I squirmed on the chair as the hard brocade seat became more and more uncomfortable. My legs were too short to reach the floor or hang over the side and I sat there, legs stuck straight out like two broomsticks. The cookies had not been served as yet and I began to think perhaps they were not meant for us at all. I slid off of the chair and walked over to momma. She and Mrs. Nasis were in deep conversation, both talking at the same time, hands gesturing wildly as they accentuated their stories. I stood next to momma hoping she would stop talking and look at me. She did not. I lightly tapped her on the shoulder and finally got her attention. I bent my head close to her ear and whispered loudly, "I want to go home. I don't have anything to do here."

Momma glared at me, silently warning me to get back up on the chair and to stay there until the visit was over. I began to whine and she placed her hand over my mouth to squelch any effort on my part to make it known how boring I thought all of this was.

"Is anything wrong, Maria?" asked Mrs. Nasis. "What does she want?" Does she have to go to the bathroom?"

"No, no, it's nothing," momma replied.

"I'm bored," I screamed. "I want to go home," I wailed.

"Oh dear, oh dear," lamented kind Mrs. Nasis. "The poor child is right. It is boring listening to two women chattering." She got up and walked over to me and offered her hand.

"Come with me," she said. I placed my hand in hers and walked into the next room. "Look, do you think you'd like to sit in here? I'll give you a plate of cookies, some milk and some picture books and you can stay here as long as you like."

Her gentle tone and genuine concern soothed me and I weighed the pros and cons of what she was offering. I looked at the little wooden rocking chair in the corner, next to a small table covered with picture books. I conceded. "Yep," I said, "I want to rock. And .. and…what kind of cookies do you have?"

Mrs. Nasis laughed as she plopped me onto the rocking chair and gave it a gentle push. She gathered books and brought them closer to me. “And now,” she announced, “time for the cookies and milk. You do have to drink all your milk, though,” she asserted.

My eyes glowed with happiness as I rocked, read and ate to my heart’s content. The little chair fitted me perfectly and the rocking back and forth soothed me and pleasured me. Time was not of the essence. I was quite content.

The clock in the hallway boomed and announced the hour. I heard momma say, “Oh, my goodness, I didn’t know it was this late. We have to leave. I must get dinner ready for Christos.”

Mrs. Nasis murmured her assurance that we could stay as long as we liked but momma insisted we had overstayed our welcome. I continued rocking and munching the last of the cookies. Momma came over to me and stopped the chair. She grasped my hand and pulled me up out of the rocker and informed me we had to hurry home as daddy would be coming home soon.

“No! No!,” I screamed. “I want to rock some more.” I plopped back down onto the rocking chair and began to propel myself backwards and forwards in a frenzy. I stuffed the last bit of cookie in my mouth and shook my head in an emphatic “No!”

“Stella,” warned momma in her sternest voice. “Let’s go. You know you can’t stay here.” She stood before me, daring me to rock one more time.

I rocked.

She grabbed me an pulled me straight up and out of the chair. She pushed me forward towards the hallway and the front door. “Now,” she hissed. “Now; we are going HOME!”

Mrs. Nasis watched the scenario unfolding before her. Her children were grown and she had long forgotten childhood tantrums. She was in awe at the force and momentum of my fury. “I want my chair; the chair; the rocking chair!" I pulled away from momma and darted back into the other room and to the waiting chair. I sat in it and began to rock as the chair creaked and cracked under the speed I was generating.

Momma charged into the room, yanked me out of the chair and onto the floor. She lifted the skirt of the sailor dress and began to whack my bottom. Mrs. Nasis stood in horrified amazement and knew not what to do.

"Maria, Maria," she began. "Don't spank her. Take the chair. Take the chair home. We don't need it. Take it. My children are grown; please take it."

I jumped up and grabbed the chair by the back and started to drag it out of the room. "Mine," I announced triumphantly, "Mine."

Needless to say the chair stayed where I had found it. Momma and I made our way home with only a few stops for more wallops on my backside. Another visit to Mrs. Nasis never took place and the little rocking chair remained there in the corner gathering dust. Perhaps that is why to this day I love rocking chairs.

My father was considered "rich". He sported a new car, expensive suits and a roll of money. Because of the show of wealth, he was asked to be the best man in many a wedding. By custom, the best man was expected to pay for a large part of the wedding paraphernalia and my father never turned anyone down. He was the honored best man, my mother was bestowed the title of Matron of Honor and I was always the flower girl. We were much in demand.

MEMBER OF THE WEDDING

"Hurry, hurry," momma reminded me. We were due at the photographer's studio in thirty minutes and I was still running around in my new petticoat. It was a pale cream silk petticoat with embroidered rose buds on the neckline and part of the outfit I was to wear as the flower girl. This was my first time in a wedding and I was very happy. My appearance as a member of the wedding party was quite the social coup for my family and excitement reigned high. The official wedding party photographs were to be taken at the studio an hour before the wedding and we had no time to waste.

Momma grabbed my arm as I whizzed by, warning me I had to get dressed. The dress was lifted gently from the box, its folds softly falling into place. Momma had designed it and momma had sewn it. It was pale yellow, with a yellow satin sash trailing silky tendrils down the back. A matching headband, adorned with blue and yellow silk flowers, was to top my curls-for-the-day. A small wicker basket filled with yellow rose petals was to loop over my left arm, leaving my right arm free to float the rose petals down the church aisle. I struggled into the dress, yards of material imprisoning me, until I could poke my head and arms through the proper openings. The bodice was straightened across my torso, the skirt fluffed around me and the headband nestled into my glistening curls. Momma stepped back to admire the product of her handiwork. She gleamed with self-satisfaction and gave one last fluff to the dress. Perfect!

Momma and daddy were also resplendent in their attire. Daddy wore his best dark gray suit and momma was so beautiful in her burgundy lace dress. The three of us emerged from the house and into the waiting Oldsmobile. My friends stood on the sidewalk and snickered as I walked by, pointing at my fancy attire and curling-iron induced curls. I quickly stuck out my tongue at them and holding my head high, flounced into the back seat of the car.

We arrived at the photography studio as the bridal party was ascending the stairs into the studio. I had never seen a bride before and I stared in awe at this royal princess in a cloud of white lace. She was so beautiful.

I sat there in silent reverence watching the group as they disappeared into the studio, mesmerized at the beautiful sight. Momma jiggled my arm, snapping me to attention, and quickly helped me hop out of the back seat of the car. I shifted from side to side, cascading the dress around me and waited for momma and daddy to help me up the steps into the studio.

This was getting tiresome. Thirty minutes of picture after picture, pose after pose. It was hot and stuffy. The bright lights of the studio only added to the oppressive heat . I had to go to the bathroom. I was hungry. I was thirsty. I was bored.

"One more," the photographer promised, "one more." I gave him a hard, steady look. "Yeah, sure," I muttered. The flash did not go off this time and the photographer cursed under his breath. He scurried off to find another flash attachment as the bridal party remained in its rigid pose, afraid to move. I started to break away. Momma grabbed me by the sash and pulled me back into place. By now my curls had wilted, the rose I was holding had withered and my skirt of many flounces now drooped in limp folds against my sweaty body. Enough of this, I thought. I walked away in search of an open window for air. I was not going to stand still for another minute. The others in the group were by now busy talking during the break and oblivious to my defection.

A new flash was soon installed. The group was rearranged into yet another pose. The photographer was ready to shoot the final picture when my disappearance was noticed.

"Where's Stella?", the bride asked, looking around wildly. My mother stepped away from the group and circled the room, frantically calling my name, overwrought with emotion and the heat of the day.

"Stella....Stella; Stella, answer me; where are you?" No response. She entered and exited two more studio rooms with no sighting of the missing flower girl. In desperation she headed for the entry hallway, silently praying that I would soon be found.

The front door to the studio was slightly ajar and a faint breeze filtered through the narrow opening. I stood there, holding my hair up with one hand and with the other fanned the yellow tulle skirt back and forth, back and forth, creating a small breeze against my perspiration-glazed legs. Ahhhhhh, bliss!, I thought, as I waved my skirt wildly. My single rose bouquet had been tossed carelessly on a nearby chair, slowly wilting and fading into a brown shadow of its former self. Momma lunged towards me, pulling me away from the sacred breeze.

"What do you think you are doing?", she hissed in her most menacing voice.

"Getting cool," I said, staring steadfastly into her fire and brimstone eyes.

"Inside," she warned. "Inside, right now."

I picked up the rose, fluffed my skirt and rearranged my now straight and sweat-soaked hair. "I'm ready," I announced, haughtily bouncing my way back to the hostile group awaiting my return.

"Okay, poses everyone," the photographer announced. "Last shot," he promised. "Straighten up in the back there. Groom, step closer to the bride. Okay; okay; looking good. Flower girl, stand up straight and smile." I glared at him, quickly grabbing my one-rose bouquet, bringing it front and center, and with it a handful of yellow tulle skirt. Pop, pop, went the flash. The final picture had been taken. The torture session was over.

****

This group picture is the most cherished one. I stand there, scowling at the photographer and the world beyond. One-rose bouquet and tulle skirt grasped with two hands, hem raised displaying my bare and scarred knees, a flower girl immortalized.

left to right- Daddy, Alex, Tassa, Momma, me, the petulant flower girl

As was the norm, fathers worked all day and played cards and drank coffee long into the night. Mothers did the housework, cooked and took care of the children. Other than visiting friends, there wasn't much for them to do for fun and relaxation. They did not drive, they would not eat in restaurants without their husbands and a social life was rather restricted - it just wasn't done and they never questioned it.

As a constant presence, I was often my mother's friend for a trip to the drugstore soda fountain or the early matinee at the neighborhood movie house. Purchase of a ticket also entitled one to a glass dish, so this was not considered a frivolous adventure; it was practical and the "free dishes were piling up high. Depression glass is now collector's item, but then it was just a bonus to an afternoon at the movies.

THE LAST PICTURE SHOW

The line moved slowly. Twenty minutes remained before the matinee was to begin and we didn't have our tickets. Momma had promised me an afternoon at the movies to see my favorite star, Shirley Temple, but the line was long and progress was slow. I tugged at momma's skirt, questioning our success. She assured me we would be seated in time.

Inch by inch, we moved closer and closer to the ticket counter, finally reaching our destination. I crossed my fingers for good luck, shut my eyes and sent a fervent prayer heavenward that we be granted our tickets. Momma counted out the money and soon two tickets were ours. Momma quickly made her way through the waiting crowd, pulling me behind her as we entered the theater lobby. I stared in awe at the ornate ceiling, the plush carpeting and the burgundy folds of the heavy drapes surrounding the lobby. This was my first time at the Rajah movie house and I was overwhelmed by its size, its beauty and its splendor. People were circling around us looking for the nearest entrance to the seating area. The movie was soon to begin.

I followed momma and mentally prepared myself to sit still for the next two hours. It would be difficult, but I would concentrate on watching Shirley Temple on the big screen. I made one pirouette, twirling my new pink organdy dress out around my scarred and bandaged knees. I clutched the bag of candy that would nourish me for the duration of the film and followed momma through the lobby.

Suddenly, I spotted the water fountain. A great thirst suddenly consumed me, a thirst I had to quench. "Momma," I said, "wait; I want some water." She glanced down at me, a puzzled look on her face. I pointed to the sparkling chrome fountain and started pulling momma towards it. She looked at her watch and cautioned me that we did not have more than five minutes. No matter, I was thirsty; I had to have water.

I wasn't tall enough to reach the flow of water from the fountain spout and there was no stepstool in sight. As momma bent to lift me high enough to meet the swirling water, I spotted a paper cup dispenser. "Momma, a cup!"

She lowered me and as my feet touched the carpeting, she led me to the gleaming chrome cup dispenser. She tugged and pulled but no cup was forthcoming. It was soon clear that money was required. One penny for one cup. Momma frantically searched through a vast coin collection on the bottom of her purse, but not a penny was to be found. Nickels, dimes, quarters, but no pennies. I insisted I had to have a cup for the water to quench my parched throat. Momma whispered her financial status and promised me a soda at the corner drugstore after the movie. That would not do. I wanted a cup for water. Again, momma tried to quiet me with pleas and promises. There was no available penny she said and reminded me that the movie was about to start.

I looked around me. People were still coming in but the lights were dimming on and off, alerting everyone that the feature was about to begin. Momma pulled me along. Suddenly I fell, crumbling onto the soft carpeting. I stretched out lengthwise, arms and legs flailing wildly, screaming for water in a little cup. Momma was embarrassed; she was angry; she was frustrated. She tried to lift me, but my body was a rigid form of pink organdy. She tried to pull me but I was dead weight. A crowd began to form around us and people were whispering and pointing. Realizing I now had an audience, my hysterics took on monumental proportions.

"Water, water; I want water," I wailed. All eyes turned on momma; cruel momma; bad momma denying her only child the water she so desperately sought.

Momma pulled me along the burgundy carpeting, leaving a matted trail of carpet fibers. I wouldn't get up and she wouldn't stop. She pulled, she tugged, she pushed and finally we were outside. Momma's breath came in spurts as she tried to regain her composure. Her dress was wrinkled and her hair was disheveled. I was prone on the sidewalk in my pink organdy splendor. Momma jerked me to my feet and I felt myself being propelled forward. Her anger was now at the danger level and I recognized the warning signals. She swatted my backside but the blows were softened by pink organdy ruffles. She pinched my legs wherever she could grab some flesh. She cursed the day she got married. She questioned the good Lord above as to His reason for giving me to her. She swatted, she pinched, she pulled, she pushed and thus we made our way home.

I ran inside and jumped onto my daddy's lap. He was my protector, my refuge, my armor against momma's wrath. Encircled in daddy's arms, I looked up at him as a big tear slowly slid down my cheek.

"Daddy," I whimpered, "Momma wouldn't get me water and I was so thirsty." And I cried more tears.

"Maria," daddy questioned, "why wouldn't you give her water? How could you do that?"

I snickered behind my hands, wiping the tears streaming down my face. Momma was in big trouble now.

Makeup was frowned upon. My mother would pinch her cheeks to bring color to them and plucked her eyebrows in private. Haircuts were a special treat at the beauty parlor. A pale lipstick gloss was used for the most special occasions, with a dusting of neutral powder to diminish the sheen of a shiny nose. And nail polish was definitely prohibited. The younger generation, however, was breaking all the rules.

FASHION MATTERS, NO MATTER THE COST!

"But daddy, EVERYBODY has them!", I informed him, waving newly polished ruby red fingernails in the air.

"I don't care. My daughter is not everybody else. No red fingernails!", he roared. "Off, take that stuff off!"

I shuffled away, gazing at my nails, admiring their ruby red glow. I was the first to flaunt red fingernails on my block and I was not about to give up my title as a fashion trend-setter. I was four years old.

I searched for momma and found her in the back yard planting her favorite flowers. Momma was a hard worker. Momma had no time for red nails. Perhaps, though, she could understand my longing for this taste of the exotic. I stopped next to momma, fingering the dirt, letting it sift through my fingers, red nails flashing amidst the dust. I sighed and looked down in deep despair. Momma put the little shovel aside and turned to face me. She lifted my chin with her hand and looked into my eyes, twin pools of sadness.

"What's wrong?", she asked. "What did you do now?"

"Nothing," I vehemently challenged her, "Nothing."

Then I sobbed. "Look," I said, holding up my dusty fingers, ruby red tips sparkling in the sunshine.

"How pretty," momma said. "Where did you get the polish?"

"Kally's sister, Penny," I volunteered."Penny did it."

"So, what's the problem?", she asked.

I whimpered and sighed and eventually responded. "Daddy won't let me keep the red; he wants it off.". With that, a loud howl penetrated the backyard silence.

"Shhhhh; shhhhhhh," momma said. "We have to do what daddy says."

"NO!", I yelled. "NO! EVERYBODY has red nails. I want them, too!"

Momma slowly raised herself from a kneeling position, dusting her hands off, sending dust particles flying in the breeze. "I'll talk to daddy," she promised, "but first, you have to take that polish off."

I put my fingers out one at a time as Penny eliminated the polish with cotton balls saturated with polish remover. One by one, the color disappeared and one by one, my nails returned to their natural no-color. How ugly, I thought. I can't wait until I grow up and can do whatever I want. I'll have the longest, reddest nails in the world, I promised myself. Sullenly I returned home, a colorless beauty.

I showed my hands to daddy. He approved. I retreated to my room to languish in misery, prepared to waste away in sadness until I was old enough to have red nails. I did not go down for dinner and I balked at my bath. I was wallowing in despair.

Momma, as a woman, was sympathetic to my beauty needs. As a mother, she had to set guidelines. As a wife, she had to respect her husband's wishes. But I didn't care. I wanted ruby red nails. As she bathed me, tears ran down my cheeks. I gazed at my nude nails, gulping in loud sobs at my loss. Momma dried me off, wrapping me in a fuzzy white bath towel. She fitted me into my favorite pajamas, the pink ones with "Good Night" written all over them. I loved those pajamas and my spirits soared somewhat. Momma kissed me and tucked me into bed, wiping the most recent tears from my eyes.

Suddenly, the door opened and the hall light flooded into my room. Daddy stood there and I scrunched down under the comforter, not knowing what to expect.

“Get up,” he said. “I have a surprise for you.” I slowly crept out of bed, found my slippers and trotted behind him, down the stairs and into the dining room. There sat momma, a towel over one end of the lace tablecloth that covered the dining room table.

“Manicure time,” she said, as daddy led me to the chair next to her. She buffed my nails. She trimmed my nails. She then turned to daddy. “Okay, now you do the rest,” she told him.

He pulled out the mercurochrome bottle and began painting my nails, one by one, with the glass stopper dripping red mercurochrome over everything. Soon I had the prettiest, most different nails of anyone. Ruby red nails were mine once again, with daddy’s blessing. I kissed him and momma and ambled back to my room. I crawled back into my bed, careful not to smudge my new ruby red nails.

****

And that explains my long, ruby red nails to this day!

My occasional outings alone with my father were the highlight of my young life. A trip to the corner ice cream parlor or a ride to the park to feed the ducks were trips to be remembered. This particular outing is to be remembered for its own specialness.

SPLENDOR IN THE SNOW

It was a cold and dreary December Saturday. The radiators were working full force, hissing and wheezing, doing their best to keep the house warm. Oatmeal bubbled on the stove and the smell of hot cocoa wafted through the kitchen. Sunlight filtered through the frost-painted windows, lukewarm rays sneaking their way into the corners of the kitchen.

Momma stirred the oatmeal and poured a small amount into a bowl, adding pats of butter and sprinkles of sugar. She placed it before me, tying a napkin around my neck and reminded me to eat all of my breakfast. Hot cocoa was in my favorite cup and I gave it a few swirls to cool it down. I began to eat as I formulated the day's plans in my mind. I knew momma would not let me play outside in the cold. Maybe someone would come over to play. Maybe momma would tell me new stories. Maybe I could listen to the radio with daddy. There were many possibilities for this cold December day.

Daddy came in and sat in his chair at the head of the table. He unfolded the newspaper and began his daily morning ritual of absorbing the events of the world. I knew not to talk to him until he had his first cup of morning coffee. I continued to be absorbed with my own nutrition but kept a careful eye on him, waiting for the very moment when I could speak. Momma placed his coffee before him and he began to sip. With a big sigh, the first gulp went down, working its caffeine wonders on him. Momma smiled and I grinned back at her. Two more swallows and he would be ready for the day.

Before I could begin my dialogue, momma presented her dilemma to him. "I have so much to do today. I have to bake, I have to cook and I must finish sewing Stella's dress. I have to finish cleaning the house…." Daddy continued reading. "And," she continued, I can't have Stella underfoot all day."

Daddy continued to read. I stopped in mid-swallow. What did she mean? I looked at her and then glanced at daddy. I waited. "Chris," she said, "I need today, all day, to do everything. Can you take Stella to the movies?" I perked up. This was going to be a better day than I had expected. I reached over and tapped daddy's hand. He looked up and I nodded towards momma, silently signaling him to listen carefully. Momma again repeated her request, punctuating it with her most beguiling smile. "Okay?", she asked.

Daddy folded the paper, looked at his watch and sighed. "Okay; we'll go to the movie. But be ready by one o'clock, Stella." With that, he pushed his chair aside and walked into the living room to his favorite chair by the window.

Momma helped me get dressed as I shivered in my underwear and socks, hopping from one foot to the other trying to keep warm. She pulled a blue sweater over my head and tugged the blue corduroy pants up, securing the belt into place. I ran downstairs. I was ready for the movie outing. My white rabbit fur coat was my choice for the day. It had a matching hat and muff that would keep me sheltered from the wintry blasts outside. I struggled into it, buttoning it snugly up to my chin. Momma adjusted the hat, tying the grosgrain ribbon under my chin in a jaunty bow. She gave me the muff after slipping a few coins into the zippered compartment for my candy treats. I waited for daddy, impatiently tapping my booted feet on the hardwood floor, sending a frantic message to daddy. He pulled himself up from the comforts of his chair, struggled into his overcoat, placed his favorite fedora on his head and took me by the hand. Momma beamed with relief. Daddy frowned in despair. I grinned in ecstasy.

I quickly jumped into the front seat of daddy's car, a big, gray Oldsmobile. Daddy turned on the ignition and steered the car slowly out of its frozen exile. We moved slowly down the icy street. I squirmed and fidgeted, anxious for an afternoon at the movies. He glanced at me and said, "Why don't I take you to Kally's house? You can play with her and her sisters. We can go to the movies another day, with momma, too, okay?"

I frowned. The choice was a difficult one. I loved going to Kally's house. She had lots of sisters and a daddy who looked like Santa Clause and who gave me nickels. She had a momma who made the best cookies. Her house was big and noisy and full of toys and people. What should I do? I pondered. I considered the many pros and cons. Kally's house it was. I told daddy and I heard what sounded like the heavy whoosh of a sigh of relief......or was that just the winter breeze whistling by the car? He turned the car around and headed back towards Kally's house.

Once there, I ran up the porch steps and into their living room, announcing my presence with my very best yell. "I'm here!!!!!" Helter-skelter, everyone came running from every which way. Kally, her sisters, her momma and poppa. Everyone circled around us, welcoming us, kissing me, admiring me in my white furry splendor. Daddy told them he would be back in a few hours. He kissed me and warned me to be good, gave silent thanks for this reprieve and quickly departed.

Kally was dressed for the outdoors. She had a game of hide and seek planned with her friends and invited me to join them, eyeing me cautiously in my finery. There she was, in a heavy snowsuit, sturdy galoshes and warm earmuffs. I stood there in white bunny fur brilliance. So what, I thought. I was ready to be one of the gang and so, off we went.

We ran, we hid, we shrieked. We stopped for sustenance - milk, scrambled egg sandwiches and cookies. Energized, we ran off again. We chose another territory to discover, the alleyway behind Kally's house. We bolted around the back, slipping and sliding in the accumulated slush. It was now my turn to be "It." I hid my eyes behind my mittened hands as I counted. "One....two....three.....four; here I come!", I warned and off I went to find my missing friends.

I ran, I scampered, I walked, carefully searching all the wondrous hiding places. I spied Kally's red-coated back as she scrunched behind a large trash can. I ran with full force and proceeded to fall into the largest mud puddle I had ever encountered. Plop! Splat! I was now face down and slithering from side to side in the slush. I heard

Kally screaming, with the others joining in a wailing chorus. I struggled to stand upright and failed with every attempt. I went down again and again. Kally and Lillian finally grabbed me by my arms and extracted me from the muddy depths. I stood up and started walking towards Kally's house, brushing and smearing the muddy sludge on my fur coat. I was frozen; I was dirty; I was a disaster; I was in big trouble.

Two hot chocolates later, daddy arrived to take me home. Kally's momma was in anguish not knowing how to tell him of the day's mishap. The coat was now a streaked chocolate brown. The hat was splattered. The muff was a matted mass of fluff. Daddy took the news well. Actually, he had a huge laugh over it as he enjoyed the coffee and cookies he had been served. I looked at him, examining every facial feature to be sure the laughter was genuine. Yep; he was not worried.

It was time to go home. It was time to face momma. I begged daddy to let me stay at Kally's, but to no avail. I struggled into my coat, now a stiff, brown "thing" and swinging my hat from the grosgrain ribbon with one hand and clutching the muff with the other, I made my way grandly back into the waiting Oldsmobile.

Daddy smiled as he patted me on top of my head.....that, too, was mud splattered....and he told me it was all right. As long as I had had a good time, I was not to worry. He parked the car and I waited for him to open my door and help me out. I slithered out, leaving a muddy trail on the gray velour seat and jumped onto the sidewalk Daddy took my hand and we walked into the house, united in our defense against the wrath and exasperation that awaited us.

"We're home," he yelled, slamming the door shut against the wailing winter wind. "We're back; where are you?"

Momma came out from the warm depths of the kitchen. Wonderful spicy aromas followed her. She looked calm; she looked relaxed....and then, "Oh, my God!", she screamed. "Chris, what did you do to the child?" I perked up, as daddy was the one in trouble, not

I! "Where did you go?"

"To Kally's," I promptly replied. "Daddy took me to Kally's!"

Momma yanked off my coat, grabbed the hat and muff and threw the entire muddy mess down the basement steps. They landed in a scruffy pile, awaiting whatever remedies momma would concoct to restore them to their former brilliance. Meanwhile, serious business was at hand. She led me into the bathroom and started filling the tub. Another bath, I thought? I had one that morning. Momma was serious and this was not the time to question her actions. "Sit there and wait," she said, pointing to the step stool. She bustled out in a frenzied search for my daddy. I heard her raised voice, the burst of anger; and daddy's attempts at a response. More raised voices. Silence. Laughter. And I sat on the little wooden step stool and waited and wondered what would ever happen to my white bunny fur coat.

It all turned out to be a most wonderful day. I had survived it without a spanking or even a lecture. I was tucked into bed early with my favorite picture books and a cup of hot cocoa. It had been a wonderful day.

Christmas was a much anticipated holiday in our house. In addition to the weekly letters to Santa Claus and daily tears of anticipation as the days until Christmas were counted down, Christmas Day was a day of great celebration. It was my father's nameday, and in keeping with Greek tradition, it was a day of welcoming friends as they came to visit and wish my father "Chronia Pola" (here's to many years) on his nameday.

Momma not only had the multitude tasks of preparing the house for the Christmas holiday, cooking and baking the many special pastries, she had to ready the house for the multitude of visitors that would descend on Christmas Day evening to wish my father their best. So Christmas, in my estimation, had to be pushed forward and my father, more of a child at heart than I, went along with the plan.

ALMOST CHRISTMAS

If only I could be good for a few more hours. If only I could get through the rest of the day with no mischief or mishap.

It was Christmas Eve afternoon, the most difficult day of the year for me to endure. I had to be good and I had to stay clean. I had to listen to momma and daddy. I had to go to bed when told. Could I? Would I?

Letters to Santa had been sent weeks ago. Remembering the many toys I had asked for, I decided I had to do as I was told. And so, I sat and waited.

Momma had spent days cleaning the house. The chandelier in the living room sent rainbow sparkles throughout the room as sunbeams bounced off of the millions of crystal pieces. The fireplace had been scrubbed clean and new logs waited to be lit. The Christmas tree was poised and waiting in the corner for Santa and his helpers to decorate. Momma had dusted, polished, mopped and vacuumed in anticipation of the holiday. Pastries and cookies had been baked and placed in the pantry to stay cool and fresh. The aroma of roasting lamb wafted through the house, mingling with the scent of lemon furniture polish, the honey fragrance of pastries and the pine scent of the Christmas tree. It was a delicious time of year and my favorite, despite the many rules and restrictions.

I was agitated, anxious and apprehensive. I didn't know how I would get through the evening, let alone sleep until morning. I envisioned the many toys and presents under the tree the next morning. The excitement was just too much for me to bear. "Is it time yet?" I would ask, only to be told to be patient a little longer. I sat in the kitchen and watched momma as she worked feverishly and I wiped away tears of frustration as the intensity of the waiting overwhelmed me.

Daddy walked into the kitchen and surveyed the scene before him.

Momma's workshop, he called it. Momma rushed from stove to sink to pantry and back again, oblivious to my misery. I jumped up and ran to him in search of solace and comfort. "I can't wait, daddy," I wailed. "It's too long. I want it to be Christmas now!"

Daddy smiled gently at me as he pondered the situation. My gaze never left his face as I waited for the solution I knew would come.

"Okay," he said, "here's what we'll do. Maria, come here and listen. We're going to play a trick on Santa Claus. We're going to make Christmas happen early!"

"What?" momma asked. A pot she was scrubbing fell from her hands and clattered into the sink. "I don't have time for nonsense. What are you thinking of?"

"Well, we'll fool Santa. We'll turn off all the lights and pretend we're sleeping. That way, Santa will think we're in bed and he'll come here first!"

I jumped up and down with joy and clapped my hands. Christmas would come early to 46 Buttonwood Street. We would fool Santa Claus!

Momma turned back to washing dishes without a word. Daddy took me in his arms and walked upstairs to my room. I promised I would wash my face, brush my teeth and change into my pajamas if he would just wait for me. He nodded.

I rushed into the bathroom and slammed the door shut for ultimate privacy. I splashed cold water on my face, squirted toothpaste on my pink toothbrush and quickly swiped the brush across my pearly whites. Sweater, overalls and underwear went into the hamper and clean pajamas enveloped me. I pattered back to the bedroom and jumped onto my bed and snuggled under the pink comforter. "Okay, turn the lights out, daddy - all of them; every one, everywhere!"

Daddy bent over to kiss me goodnight and patted me on the head.

"Okay, eyes shut tight. No peeping. I'll turn all the lights off up here and momma and I will be in the kitchen. Remember, don't get up until we tell you."

"But daddy, Santa will see the lights on in the kitchen," I lamented.

"No, no. The kitchen is in back of the house and hard to see. The fireplace is in the living room and it will be very, very dark. Don't worry, Santa will never know."

With that he closed the bedroom door and went downstairs to join momma, who was still working away in the brightly lit kitchen.

I stared at the ceiling and watched shadows from the tree branches as they swayed across the ceiling and walls. I tossed and turned and stayed silent as I waited for Santa to come.

Next thing I knew, there was daddy by my bed. He was shaking me awake and saying, "Stella, Stella, get up! I think Santa came."

"You think?" I questioned.

"Yes, I think I heard bells jingling and reindeer hooves. I think we really fooled Santa."

Without waiting for help, I tossed the bedcovers off and ran out of the bedroom. There was no time for robe and slippers. I had to see this miracle for myself.

I ran down the spiral staircase and stopped midway at my favorite vantage point. I peered over the railing and gazed into the living room. The tree was ablaze with lights of all colors. Mounds of presents were stacked under the tree; so many, it would take hours to open them all. I plopped down on the stair and squirmed into a comfortable spot on the soft carpeting. I was too excited to go any further. Daddy joined momma in the living room and they stood there looking up at me. They smiled and beckoned for me to join them in the living room.

I was laughing and crying at the same time. I was sobbing and hiccuping, emotions running riot within me. I continued down the remaining stairs and went into the living room. I gazed in silent awe at the splendid tree. I sat down and began to poke through the many boxes, shaking each one as I tried to guess what it held. I was still crying and laughing at the same time as I began to open my presents. We had really fooled Santa Claus!

"Hmmm, I wonder if we can fool Santa again next year?"

Greek housewives took great pride in a clean and tidy home. With brooms and mops, carpet beaters and dust cloths, they waged war on the daily dust and grime. I was soon to be initiated into the tradition.

CLEANING 101

I was beginning to think momma was "clean crazy." Every Saturday she cleaned the house. From top to bottom, she cleaned the house. She dusted, scrubbed, mopped, washed, waxed, polished and vacuumed. Every Saturday! Didn't she have anything better to do, I would wonder?

Another Saturday and momma was once again in another frenzy of cleaning. I was confined to the house because of the nasty weather and I soon ran out of things to do for entertainment. I followed momma downstairs as she bounced the vacuum cleaner down each step. "Momma," I lamented, "I have nothing to do. I'm bored."

"Humph," she muttered. "I wish I could be bored for once." She plugged in the vacuum cleaner and it roared to life. She guided it here, there and everywhere, leaving wide swaths of clean carpet in its wake. I followed as she made her attack on each room.

Suddenly she stopped the vacuum cleaner in mid "whir-rrrr." She snatched a cloth from her apron pocket and tossed it towards me. She handed me a bottle of furniture polish. "So, you're bored? Well, here's something you can learn to do today. You can dust and polish the furniture. You're old enough to help now."

She guided me towards the dining room and told me to start in there. When that was finished, I was to move on into the living room. I gazed at the massive table and six chairs. The china closet loomed against the far wall. A chest of drawers took up space on the near wall, topped with crystal candlesticks and various knickknacks. In back a large mirror hung on the wall, surrounded by an ornate gold frame.

"Everything has to be dusted; everything," she instructed me. "The table legs are carved and have many ridges. You have to dust inside each curve, so do a good job. Then, you can do the living room. You will be a big help to me today."

I balled up the dustcloth and proceeded to dust. At first, it was fun seeing the white film of dust disappear and the gleaming wood shine through. But it quickly became evident that as soon as I dusted, the dust resettled. I saturated the cloth with the polish and ran around and around the table, quickly dissolving the white dust. There, I thought, that takes care of the dust.

I crawled under the table to dust the table legs. There before me were four intricately carved table legs and a middle pedestal. There were grooves and niches everywhere, all coated with dust. I wrapped the end of the dustcloth around my index finger and proceeded to clean the first of many ridges.

"Stella, where are you? Are you finished yet?" Momma entered the dining room through the swinging door from the kitchen and circled the room. "Where are you?" she asked again, her voice becoming slightly agitated.

There I was, huddled under the table, slowly dusting each narrow groove as tears slid down my face. I was dusting the second table leg and by now was totally frustrated. I was tired and more bored than I had ever been in my life. I heard momma calling me again and I called out to her, sobbing, "I'm under here."

Momma bent down and peered under the table. She watched as I dusted the table legs, occasionally wiping my cascading tears with the dustcloth. "Come out," she commanded.

I crawled out into the daylight of the dining room. I threw the dustcloth on the floor and dropped the furniture polish bottle next to it. "I'm not finished, but I don't want to finish. I don't like dusting and you can't make me!"

I ran out of the dining room and upstairs to my bedroom, my sanctuary. I picked up a coloring book and began to color, oblivious to the work that still had to be done.

"Boy," I murmured, "I'll never have all those curves and curlicues in my furniture when I grow up."

I continued coloring. I was no longer bored.

****

Next time you come to my house, please note how straight all of the furniture legs are. There's a reason.

My father catered to my every whim. My great desire for "Shirley Temple curls" resulted in my first beauty parlor experience.

PERMANENT STATUS

"No, no!" I wailed. "Don't touch my curls! No!"

Every morning, the same lament. Every morning momma would try to comb my hair. Every morning I fought to keep my "curls."

You see, I had stick-straight hair. Shiny, black, straight hair in the traditional bowl cut with bangs. No curls, no waves, just stick-straight hair.

But every morning I had "curls" ("pillow hair" - like "hat hair," only worse!). I had tangles and knots but in my mind, I had curls. And they were not to be messed with.

I cringed as momma would come towards me, comb in hand. She had learned over time to block the door and grab me as I raced round the room in search of an escape route. She would grab me, push me down on the little chair by the window and begin wielding the comb. She would pull and yank and jerk my hair to my accompanying wails of pain and distress.

One particular morning, a Sunday, I was especially protective of my curls. I was sprawled under the bed, defying momma to come and get me. After many futile attempts, momma threw the comb on the floor and slammed my bedroom door shut. I listened for her footsteps going down the stairs. Once assured she was not nearby, I emerged. I gazed into the triple-mirror on the dresser and ruffled my hands through my hair. I fluffed the tangles and admired my "curls."

I ventured downstairs, still a bit wary of momma's unfinished efforts. I tiptoed into the living room and over to the big chair where daddy sat reading the paper. I stood before him, not speaking, not certain if he had had his quota of morning coffee. He glanced at me and slowly lowered the paper. I waited.

"Well, now," he said, "what are you still doing in pajamas"? And what's the matter with your hair?"

I began to cry.

Momma hurried in to see what was happening to disrupt a quiet Sunday morning. One look at me and she strongly suggested I get the comb.

I jumped into daddy's lap and nestled my head against his massive chest, seeking comfort and protection. "NO!" I yelped. I placed my hands over my head, protecting the precious "curls" and raced out of the room, back upstairs to my bedroom. There I stayed for the rest of the day.

Monday dawned and another battle waited to be fought. Momma, however, made no attempt to comb my hair. She selected a dress from my closet, tossed clean undershirt, panties and socks on the bed and ordered me to get dressed. I did, for there was no threatening comb in sight.

She followed me downstairs and guided me into the kitchen for the waiting bowl of oatmeal. I sat and ate in silence, "curls" intact, but with great doubts forming.

"We're going to Froso's today," announced momma as she scraped the left-over oatmeal into the sink and ran the water into the pan to soak. "So, let's go now so we won't be late." I knew Froso as a friend of momma's, but why were we going to see her, I wondered?

Fifteen minutes later, we entered into a world where I had never been. Froso came towards us and greeted us warmly. She tousled my hair as I screamed in protest. "See, see what I mean, Froso?" momma asked. Froso just smiled.

"Come here, Stella,' Froso beckoned. "Climb up into this big, comfortable chair."

I did and stared at myself reflected in the mirror covering the wall before me. She placed a large cape over me and snapped the buttons in the back. She selected several combs and stood behind me, ready to disposses me of my curls.

"No, don't touch my 'curls'," I hissed. I tried to wiggle out of the confines of the chair but could not.

"Stella, Stella, listen to me," begged Froso. "I'm going to give you the most beautiful curls in the world. No one will be able to comb them out. They will be all over your head, just like Shirley Temple."

I perked up.

"But first I have to comb your hair. These aren't real curls," she informed me. "These are just knots and tangles from sleeping. In just a few hours you will have Shirley Temple curls."

The lure of looking like my matinee idol was too much to resist. I gravely nodded and settled into the chair, surrounded by the cape and waited for the curls to happen.

Froso tugged and pulled and untangled every last "curl." I stared at the straightness reflected in the mirror. Daddy often told me I had hair like leeks - "prasa," in Greek - straight and split-ended. And I would cry. But now I would have curls if I would only be patient.

A smelly, cold liquid saturated my head. Froso rolled my hair on fat rollers and saturated them with more of the smelly stuff. I gazed in awe as the rods covered my head and I envisioned the curls to be. Froso told me to get up and move to another chair by the wall. I was hesitant for there was a big metal hood over the chair with long black wires dangling from it. I looked up at Froso in fear.

"Nothing to be afraid of, Stella," said Froso in a comforting tone. "I'll put a clamp over each roller and then turn on the machine. It will set your curls into permanent ones. That's what we call what we are doing - you are having a permanent wave. Do you know what that means?"

I nodded in the affirmative but I really didn't know. Froso proceeded to snap metal clamps on each and every curling rod on my head. The clamps bit down on each curling rod. The connecting wires disappeared into the metal hood overhead. I was a captive in the oversized chair, cloaked in a cape, my head connected to wires. There was no escaping now. Froso continued clamping each curl as I sat in escalating silent horror.

"There, that's done,"announced Froso. She pushed a button and a quiet hum surrounded me. I soon felt heat all over my head. My eyes widened in fear.

"Ha, ha, ha," laughed momma, pointing at me. "She looks like a miniature Medusa." She continued to laugh, joined in by Froso.

I squirmed in the chair, a victim of their humor. I didn't know who this Medusa was but if they were laughing it couldn't be a compliment. I wanted to jump out of the chair but could not as I was tethered and held tight by the many wires.

"Who's Medusa?" I questioned. "Why are you laughing at me? Get me out of here; get me out!"

I started to pull forward in the chair in an effort to escape. The wires held me back. I panicked. I screamed in fear and started unclamping the curling rods. The heat seared my fingers, escalating my screams to yet another dimension.

Froso rushed to my side, her eyes wide in a startled gaze. "Sit still, Stella. Don't get up, you'll pull all of the wires out of their sockets. Sit down; calm down!" she commanded.

I shrank back into the confines of the soft leather chair. The wires continued to hum as my curls "cooked." "I'm afraid," I admitted. "My head is hot and I can't get loose from here. I don't like this." I began to whimper.

Froso made soft cooing sounds as she patted my shoulder in an effort to unruffle me. “Ten more minutes, Stella, and you’ll have beautiful curls. Nothing will hurt you, I promise.”

“Where’s my momma? I want momma,” I cried. “I want to go home.”

Momma rushed up to me, her hair wrapped in a huge white towel. “I’m right here,” she said. “I’m having my hair washed and set. I’m just two chairs down from you. Sit still; your curls are almost done.” She kissed me and went back to her chair.

Soon I was unclamped from the mass of wires. The rods were removed and I was taken back to the shampoo room. Warm water rushed over my head and I tentatively patted my head to find the curls.

There they were! Wet as they were, I could tell I had curls. Real curls, not matted morning hair. I had curls; a million of them! My tears dried as my crying stopped. Froso rubbed my head with a fragrant cream and walked me to the dryers. I frowned, for I was not going to get hooked up to wires again.

“No, no, Stella,” replied Froso, anticipating my fear. “No wires, just nice warm air to dry your curls. Hop up on the chair and put your head under the dryer hood.”

I did as I was told. The hood came down over my head, past my eyes, blocking my view. Froso turned a knob and warm tropic air swirled about my head. I felt the curls springing to life - I really could - and I was anxious to see my finished curls. I just knew I would have even more curls than Shirley Temple.

The buzzer finally sounded, signaling the end of the drying session. I made my way out from under the dryer and walked to the styling booth. Froso was there waiting for me, brush and comb in hand. She helped me onto the chair and quickly elevated it up several inches. I liked that; this was now getting to be fun.

I looked at the image staring out at me from the wall of mirrors. My head was huge with massive curls, hundreds and hundreds of them. I grinned.

Froso began to comb out each curl, gently coaxing them into place. She didn't tug or pull and she hummed as she performed her magic on me. I shut my eyes in anticipation of the finished product.

"There, Stella, you're finished. Take a look."

She handed me a large hand mirror and spun me around in the chair. "Open your eyes and look, Stella."

I looked in the hand mirror and saw the back of my head reflected in the wall of mirrors. I had big, fat sausage-like curls all over my head. This was truly a miracle. From leek-like hair, as daddy would say, I now had glorious, shiny, bouncy, curls. I patted my head to make sure they were reality and not a dream. They were really there, the many dozens of them. I kept patting each and every one just to make sure they were still there.

Momma came up to me and gasped. "Stella, you look beautiful. You look like Shirley Temple - with more curls!"

I shook my head and curls went flying every which way. "See, see, momma, real curls."

As days went by, the same morning lament began. Every morning momma would try to convince me to have my hair combed. Every morning I fought to keep my curls intact. And so, every day momma lost the battle and I emerged victorious with a variety of matted curls and knotted curls. These were **real** curls and I wasn't about to let them go.

ΓΡΕΧΙΑΝ ΟΔΨΣΣΕΨ

(GRECIAN ODYSSEY)

In 1937, my mother and I traveled to Greece for a six-month stay. It was her longing to see her mother, sister and brothers. Looking back, I realize that marital problems were rearing their ugly head. My mother's ultimatum was a trip to Greece so she and my father could reevaluate their situation. My father granted her wish. I was to go with her and little did they know the six-month ordeal my mother and relatives were to endure.

The stories that follow are still so vivid in my memory. I was truly a spoiled brat, no other way to describe me!

ADVENTURE

I was five years old and in Greece with momma to visit my grandmother in Piraeus. This trip had not been in my plans at all and I had not come willingly. I had kicked and screamed and clung to my daddy as he bid us farewell. The ship had sailed accompanied by my shrieks of terror as we left daddy standing on the dock. Momma and I were going to Greece for a long visit. I started crying the moment we set sail and momma later would vouch that I did not stop crying for the entire six months.

Despite the trauma of being separated from my daddy, despite the daily tears and tantrums, I had random days where I forgot my longing for daddy, totally immersed in the antics of my cousins and the neighborhood children. I was as much a novelty to them as they were to me.

We had been in Piraeus for a week and I was slowly adjusting to momma's family. How strange it seemed that momma had a momma and sisters and brothers. She was a momma and she was not supposed to have anyone but me and daddy.

It was another hot, sultry day. The awnings were down, casting long shadows over the black and white tiles in the courtyard patio. A bird trilled now and then but it, too, hovered in the coolness of shadows, napping the sultry afternoon away. My grandmother, my aunt and my mother were all in their rooms settling down for the traditional afternoon siesta. Despite their combined efforts, I was not about to take a nap.

I hopped up and down the length of the patio, jumping from white tile to black tile and back to the white, up and down, up and down. Suddenly, the wrought iron gate slammed and my cousins, George and Taki, screeched their way in, breaking the silence that hovered over the patio. They, too, were searching for companionship in an effort to escape the dreaded siesta nap. Soon the three of us were hopping up and down like three little grasshoppers.

Soon tiring of this game, I sat down on the tile floor. It was hot from the overhead sun and I shot back up and relocated to a shady spot under the kitchen awning. George and Taki began jumping up, touching the awning and hitting their fingers around its perimeter. Taki then jumped a bit higher and grabbed the iron frame of the awning. He began chinning himself, all the while counting, "One…two….three"….He would drop back down, only to take another leap at the frame, trying to outdo himself. "five…six…." He lost his grip and fell. George immediately entered the competition and soon they were in active combat as to who would outnumber the other. Eight….nine….ten!

I counted as I watched them in wide-eyed wonder. How graceful; how tempting; how fun. I was too short to reach the frame; I was five years old to their ten and twelve, and I was in awe at their tremendous prowess. I was determined, however, that I, too, was going to join in this fascinating game and I would overcome all obstacles. Using all the feminine charms available at age five, I coerced them to pick me up, boost me high enough to reach the iron frame.

George, being the older of the two and taller, put his arms around my waist and lifted me up….higher and higher I went…I could now see the top of the awning and the frame support. I clutched the frame, kicking George away, swinging and twirling as I began chinning myself….one……two…..

My hands slipped. I felt myself falling, falling, falling, backwards and downwards. My head soon came into contact with the beloved black and white tile patio and my athletic endeavors ended with loud screams and blood-letting.

My grandmother, aunt and momma came scrambling out into the patio. They hovered around me, soothing me, kissing me and rubbing my head, despite the blood now gushing forth. In unison, they began chastising George and Taki, for surely it was their fault that I was lying on the ground with a gash in my head. I was in great pain, indeed, but I was also savoring the moment.

The head wound eventually healed and all ended well. No more chinning on the patio awning took place. To this day, I firmly believe there is still a dent in that old black and white tile floor in my grandmother's house in Piraeus.

passport photo-
(…note the perm!)

A TIME TO SLEEP, A TIME TO WEEP

Everything was so different here in Greece. It was hot every day and every night. People talked "funny." My cousins stared at me and brought their friends to gawk at me, the "Amerikana." My aunt smothered me constantly with kisses and my grandmother scared me. She wore black all the time and had wispy gray hair covered by a black silk scarf. Worst of all, everyone took naps every day! I hated it here!

Meeting relatives, tasting different foods, sharing momma with her sister and mother had taken their toll. I was not ready to be cordial. I missed my daddy and it was, in my opinion, cruel to take me away from him for six months. I had decided I would get even. And so, I cried every day.

It was time for the dreaded nap again. My grandmother slowly lowered the green awning, shading the patio and closed the shutters, plunging the house into a semblance of coolness. My aunt disappeared into her room and my grandmother slowly walked into the front bedroom. Momma stretched out on the bed in our designated room, plumping the pillow, pulling up the sheet, ready to spend a quiet hour or two. She motioned me towards the other bed where my pajamas were folded neatly at the foot of the bed. She suggested that I prepare for my nap. I shook my head from side to side, red barrettes flying loose, bangs flapping in my eyes. "No!," I whispered, "no nap."

Momma quickly sat up and began her descent from the high feather bed. In her bare feet she crossed the room in record speed and began to unbutton my sundress. I squirmed out of her reach and raced to the doorway and stood there, arms crossed, legs firmly braced.

"It's too hot outside now; we have to rest for a while, Stella. A short nap and then we'll go for a walk and buy some pastries; all right?"

I considered my options and decided to negotiate. I would take a nap but under my terms. No pajamas; no bed. I would rest on the cool marble floor in the living room. It was dark, quiet and cool in there. I would take my dress off and sleep in my panties and undershirt for a very short nap and then we would go to the corner pastry shop as promised. Momma sighed in relief, assuring peace for herself and the entire household. She led me by the hand to the dark interior of the living room. I selected my preferred spot and stretched out on the cool marble floor. I assured momma I would be quite comfortable without pajamas and I would keep my underpants and shirt on. I would close my eyes and I would sleep. I promised. Momma hovered, making sure I was comfortable and then tiptoed back to her room for a much needed nap.

I squirmed, I wiggled. The floor, although quite cool, was hard. I was prone on my back, legs spread out, arms outstretched, taking up as much of the cool marble floor as I could. It was so quiet; not a sound could I hear from either inside or out. The whole world was taking a nap. My shirt was soon saturated with perspiration and sticking to my paunchy stomach. I began to roll it up slowly, from the bottom up to the top, ending in a tight roll from shoulder to shoulder. That seemed cooler and my bare skin absorbed what cool air happened to trickle in through the slats of the drawn shutters. The silence was calming and my eyelids closed; opened; closed. I was getting drowsy; the stillness was hypnotic and sleep was on its way.

The door slowly creaked open. My eyes fluttered open to the sound and I turned my head towards the sound. There was my grandmother slowly gliding her way across the room to me, her youngest grandchild, to assure herself that I was comfortable, safe and sound. Her steps were hushed as she crept towards me, her carpet slippers sliding effortlessly across the slick marble floor. She knelt by me and I quickly closed my eyes, feigning sleep. I felt her hand slowly stroking my wet bangs away from my forehead. I felt her caressing my sunburned cheeks. "Sweet, sweet love," she crooned as she knelt there, staring at me. She slowly began to lower my undershirt to cover the exposed torso, to keep me from getting chilled, to keep me from getting bitten by stray mosquitoes, to make me more comfortable.

"Sweet, sweet child," she crooned as she bent to kiss me.

"MOMMA! MOMMA!", I screamed, almost toppling my grandmother over with the pure strength of the sound. "Momma! Momma! She touched me!", I wailed as my grandmother silently walked away, shaking her head, wondering how she could break the barrier between us.

I never sat in my grandmother's lap. I never let her hug me. I never really talked to her. I was resentful of the time my mother spent with her, but I never tried to spend time with her. I never became the grandchild she wanted me to be.

Years later, I regretted the times lost and apologized for the spoiled child I had been. I wrote to her, I knitted socks for her, but I never saw her again. How very sad.

THE BIG BANG

It was the Saturday before Easter. Preparations for the big holiday dinner kept the adults preoccupied. My cousins entertained themselves with games of tag. As for me? I cried.

In total frustration, my mother rushed out from the kitchen, apron awry, sandals flapping on the patio tiles, wiping her hands on a cloth towel as she walked rapidly towards me. Her face and her voice quickly told me she had too much to do to put up with the likes of me. I pursed my mouth and quickly went over to my cousins, faking sudden interest in their game. Momma came closer, her looks conveying what words would not say. She turned to my cousins and pleaded with them to do something with me, as the constant crying and whining was disrupting the entire household and the preparations for the holiday.

George and Taki pondered this request. What could they do with me? I looked at them sullenly, ready to initiate a new barrage of tears if they didn't amuse me and entertain me soon.

George put his hand in his back pocket and pulled out what looked like an old sheet of paper. Taki grinned and nodded. I stepped forward to take a closer look. They squatted on the ground and taking pieces of the paper, produced crackling, popping, magnificent sounds. This was magic paper!

I plopped down beside them, temporarily forgetting my mother's reminders to stay clean.. Momma's daily loads of laundry and the nightly scouring of my filthy knees and elbows were becoming burdensome. I brushed my bangs out of my eyes and moved in closer for an in-depth contemplation of the mystery paper.

Snaps and crackles and short flashes of sparks continued. I squiggled between George and Taki, positioning myself right up front.

"Let me, let me," I begged. They exchanged glances. Should they, they silently asked each other. George took a piece of the magic paper and placed it between his thumb and forefinger. He quickly rubbed the paper back and forth, back and forth, letting it fly loose when the first crackle was heard. The paper popped and exploded quickly, bouncing helter-skelter across the black and white patio tiles. I looked at Taki. I looked at George. I was enthralled. Tears were forgotten. Daddy was forgotten. Going home was forgotten. This was very exciting, new and different!

"Let me try…please?", I pleaded. Taki tore a small piece from the paper he held and placed it between his fingers.

"Now watch me first," he commanded and began his demonstration. I followed his every move, mesmerized. I memorized every maneuver; I was ready.

A piece of the magic paper was gently placed between my tiny fingers. Taki gently rubbed my fingers back and forth across the paper until the first crack was heard. He pulled away, yelling final instructions to me. The paper was stuck to my fingers. I couldn't shake it loose. Smells of burning flesh and scorched paper indicated that something had gone drastically wrong with the pyrotechnics.

I howled. I shook my hand but the paper was really stuck. I howled louder and louder. Taki and George retreated as fast as they could, leaving me alone with the emerging blisters. Momma rushed out once again to see what was wrong. A damp towel was quickly placed over my fingers in an effort to dislodge the paper now firmly bonded to my fingers. More howls ensued, as the audience to my disaster grew. I was showered with hugs and kisses. I howled some more. The search was on for the instigators and I covertly basked in my current moment of glory.

Punishments were doled out appropriately to George and Taki. I, on the other hand, was pampered and coddled. I continued to pierce the sound barrier for two days and two nights with yelps of pain. I swished swollen, burnt fingers in a tall glass of water which I carried

Stella and playmates in Greece

everywhere with me.

George and Taki vowed to never play with me again.

THE TOURIST

A blustery March day. Spring hovered but was reluctant to arrive. The wind whistled through the courtyard. The striped awning over the kitchen door flapped and fluttered. Leaves were torn away from the trees and sent fluttering downwards.

We were not to be daunted, however. A day trip to the Acropolis had been planned and the excitement of an outing was more forceful than any March wind. Momma had not seen the Acropolis since she was a very young girl and this would be my first glimpse of the Grecian wonder. They were eager to show us this antiquity and great efforts had been made to guarantee a wonderful day.

I, of course, didn't want to go.

Momma kept opening the kitchen door to test the velocity of the wind. Each time she announced that the weather was improving. The excursion would take place.

Momma, her mother, her sister with her fiancé, her brother Stefanos and his wife were all in high spirits over the planned picnic. Food was placed in large baskets and a taxi had been reserved for the trip up the winding road to the top of the Acropolis. Everyone bundled up in overcoats, scarves, hats and gloves and waited for the taxi to arrive. I was hiding in the bedroom I shared with momma, curled up on the small bed that had been placed in the room for me.

I heard the "beep, beep" of the taxi announcing its arrival. I heard the front door slam shut and the sounds of everyone talking at the same time. Perhaps they wouldn't notice that I was not among them.

Wriggling into a more comfortable spot on the bed, I pulled the blanket over me and relished its soothing warmth. I thumped the pillow, sending feathers fluttering towards the ceiling, and settled down for a nap.

Suddenly, I was yanked out of bed in silent fury. Momma was glaring at me and her breath was coming in short spurts. "You scared me!" she shouted. "We were ready to leave and you weren't with us. What do you think you are doing?"

My feet hit the cold marble floor and I yelped in surprise. I was in my underwear and shivering. Socks, shoes and warm clothing were thrown at me in great haste as momma commanded that I get dressed as quickly as possible. I pulled one sock on and then the other. I forced my feet into the patent leather Mary Janes and quickly buckled them. A navy blue wool dress was pulled over my head and tugged over my skinny body. A comb was raked through my hair and a bright red barrette anchored my bangs. Momma opened the creaky door to the wardrobe closet and sorted through the entangled hangers and clothes in an effort to locate my coat. There, pushed into the far corner was my pride and joy, my white bunny fur coat. Momma pulled it off the hanger and ordered me to hold out my arms as she struggled to get the coat on me.

The beep of the waiting taxi underscored the urgency the moment.. "Hurry, hurry," momma warned. "They'll leave without us if you don't hurry."

Good, I thought. I didn't want to go and the thought of being left behind was not an unpleasant one for me.

The coat was buttoned tightly all the way up to the very top button. The white wool felt hat was placed on my head and the grosgrain ribbon tied tightly under my chin. The matching white fur muff was tossed at me as momma warned me not to lose it. Although the muff had a ribbon attached to a bracelet to be worn over the wrist, I was prone to losing or forgetting it.

The taxi beeped again, louder this time. Momma snatched my hand and raced through the house and out the front door. We squeezed into the taxi and I was placed on my uncle's lap due to lack of space. He was my favorite relative and so I did not mind sitting on his lap. I grabbed his arm as the taxi bumped along the uneven roads. I managed to stay seated as we made the ascent towards the wonders of the Acropolis.

Excitement reigned high. Everyone was talking at once, pointing at the many wonders of the ancient site and the view of Athens below us. We trudged and stumbled from one ancient temple to another. A guide described each structure and its history. Momma seemed to take in every syllable and absorbed all the history around us. Everyone was in a holiday mood and seemed to be enjoying the excursion despite the chill wind. I, on the other hand, was not having a good time at all.

I tagged along beside momma, her hand firmly holding mine. She didn't let go, not even for a second. She told me I was in the very cradle of civilization and my roots went way, way back to this era. I was not impressed.

By noon the wind had diminished and the sun was slowly warming the huge rocks and boulders. My uncle announced that the group would now stop for lunch. A flat-top boulder was to be our table and the surrounding rocks our chairs. My grandmother quickly unfolded a white tablecloth and spread it over the boulder. Food emerged from the many baskets. Roasted chickens; fava beans sprinkled with olive oil and oregano; olives; cheese and large loaves of homemade bread were placed on the makeshift table.

Silence descended as the hungry group nourished itself. I found a small broken column among the rubble and sat apart from the others. I nibbled on the chicken, foregoing the fava beans. I munched on large slices of the homemade bread slathered with freshly churned butter. I was ravenous and the food was truly nectar of the gods.

My uncle began taking pictures of the temples and the surrounding scenery. He then turned towards the group and focused the camera for the best shot. I stood up abruptly and began to walk away. I did not want my picture taken today. I was not in the mood to smile. Momma grabbed me and plunked me in the middle of the group, guaranteeing that I would not take flight again.

My uncle waved to a passing tourist and asked if he would be kind enough to take a picture of our group. "Of course," he said, as he walked towards my uncle. He focused the camera and arranged the group before the Caryatids Temple. "Perfect, perfect," he muttered as he squinted through the box camera sight and prepared to snap the picture. "Everyone be still; I'm ready to take the picture. It will be a wonderful picture." Click…click.

The day ended and the taxi weaved its way down the curving roads and onto the road back to Piraeus. Everyone agreed it had been a wonderful day and the pictures would be a lasting memory to be cherished forever. Momma would have much to tell everyone when we returned home and the pictures would be looked at over and over.

The pictures were developed and my uncle rushed into the kitchen to share the fun of looking at the family gathering as captured by the camera. The pictures were scattered on the table and everyone began grabbing for a first look.

In every shot, I stood out among the group in my white bunny fur coat. In every one, my back was turned to the camera. I had made my statement. I did not want to be there.

me (center, white), in bunny fur coat, being obnoxious!

THE TOY SHOP

Three more months and the planned six-month stay in Greece would be over. I still hated being here. But momma was so happy to be with her family again and she was not about to let my tantrums ruin her visit. Three more months were to be endured.

My daily crying sent momma into a frenzy. No amount of soothing, cajoling, spoiling or scolding could bring me to a complete stop. Sobbing usually resulted in special treats, just to coax a smile onto my sullen little sun-bronzed face. Special hot cocoa was made in the morning just for me. I would tear buttered bread into a "zillion" pieces, stuffing them into the cup, watching the crumbs absorb the liquid, a dark brown mess which I would then hungrily devour. Fresh milk was provided me from the little goat tethered outside the garden gate. Entertainment was planned by my cousins - under protest - and shopping trips resulted in toy purchases. I was to be pleased, no matter the cost. I was to be silenced, no matter the price.

It was another burning, sultry hot day. The sky was its usual blinding blue, punctuated by white puffy clouds. A tiny breeze would flutter by now and then bringing some relief. Momma and her sister were in a hurry to finish their shopping before the shops closed for the customary afternoon siesta. The two of them had planned an excursion together, away from other family members. My constant whining that morning, a daily occurrence, had ceased only for the time it took me to eat my breakfast. I was stirring and sipping my "bread and chocolate concoction", leaving a liquid trail on the black and white tiles of the patio. My eyes were ever alert to everyone's movement around me. I soon sensed that momma was going on an adventure without me. I quickly swallowed the last of the cocoa and began to amble up and down the length of the patio, a sorrowful figure. I directed my most anguished look towards momma, a tear streaking its way down my chocolate-smeared cheeks.

"I miss daddy," I whimpered. I saw momma's desperate look. I could feel the guilt I had so effectively generated. I sobbed and gulped a few more times. I wiped my tear-blinded eyes and saw momma coming towards me.

Momma knelt beside me, gently rubbing my back, making soothing sounds, coaxing me to give her a smile. My chin trembled and my eyes filled with a new supply of tears. I managed a half-hearted mournful smile. I sighed again and slowly twisted my little handkerchief around and around my sticky, chocolate-stained fingers. My aunt joined us, great concern on her face. How could they possibly leave me, the forlorn little child, the homesick little girl? They had no choice. They would take me with them. I grinned in victory.

The three of us boarded the bus and headed for the shopping district. My mind whirled with the many toy possibilities and I anticipated the treasures I would bring home at the end of the afternoon. I hummed and I smiled. Momma and her sister were busy talking and plotting their shopping itinerary as I gazed out of the window at the scenery whizzing by. It was only 10 o'clock but the heat was already intolerable. The bus was stifling. My dress was stuck to the leather seat cushion. My feet were burning inside my sandals and my hair was a damp, tangled mess.

The bus came to an abrupt stop in midtown and we descended. I walked between momma and my aunt, holding tightly to their hands. Athens was a big, busy city and I didn't want to get lost. In and out, in and out, in and out we went. So many stores, so many things to look at and so many things they had to buy. I was restless as none of the stores were where I wanted to be. Shopping for clothes and household items did not interest me. I tugged momma's arm and reminded her not to forget the toy store. She patted me on the head, smoothing my tangled, sweaty bangs and assured me a visit to the toy store was definitely on the agenda. More stores, more boring things to look at and not a toy store anywhere in sight. I was tired, hot and thirsty. It was getting more and more difficult to keep up with their fast pace.

I shuffled along, stubbing my toes on the many pebbles on the sidewalk, kicking them out of the way. I sighted a street vendor on the corner selling my favorite beverage. It was only colored sugar water, but I loved it. I ran over and ordered before momma could veto my choice. The sight of flies buzzing around the sweet sugar water was not to momma's liking, but it was too late. I clutched the paper cup in triumph and looked at momma as she dug out the coins to pay. I sipped happily as we continued on our route. "Don't forget my toys," I whispered between mouthfuls of the green sugary water. I was assured the toy store would be our last stop. Happiness welled up inside me, all warm and bubbly. What a wonderful day this was turning out to be. I continued slurping green sugar water.

We turned a corner and there before us was a toy store. "Children's Palace," the sign signaled and my eyes widened in wonder at the display in the storefront windows. We walked into the dim, cool darkness of the store, our eyes slowly adjusting from the brilliance of the sun. A lavish display of toys, dolls, balls, stuffed animals, miniature cars, trains and trucks overwhelmed me. I went from one display to another, touching, holding, feeling, examining everything. I picked up a doll, a pretty one with blonde curls, blue eyes and a pink dotted swiss ruffled dress and matching hat. I held her tightly, close to my side. I grabbed a bright red ball, a shiny bugle and a fuzzy brown teddy bear, all the while looking for more treasures. I placed everything on the counter, cautioning the salesperson to keep a close watch on my toys. I found momma sitting in a chair nearby, her legs stretched out in front of her, fanning herself with a little paper fan. My aunt was doing the same in the next chair. I looked at them both, questioning the pause in the shopping spree.

"Momma," I said, "I found what I want."

"How many?", she asked. I started itemizing, holding up one finger for each item....one...two...three...four.

"What!!!!", hissed momma in a shrill whisper; "Four?" I nodded most emphatically. I guided her to the counter and proudly pointed out my choices. Four.

Momma moved her head from side to side…no,no,no. I bobbed my head up and down…yes, yes, yes. No..Yes..No…Yes! In desperation, momma priced the doll. It was too expensive. The ball was a possible choice. The bugle wasn't worth the asking price. The teddy bear would only be one more for the vast collection I had back home. The ball would have to be the toy choice for the day. I mulled over the decision. I wasn't ready to settle yet. I stood in the middle of the toy store and carefully gazed at the toy inventory around me, calculating my next choice. I saw a drum set, a beautiful red drum set, something I did not already have. I pointed and said, "That one, too. The ball and the drums." I folded my arms across my chest, standing tall and reiterated my choice. "Red ball; red drums." I waited for momma to toss the money on the counter and to ask for the toys to be wrapped. I waited and I waited. I looked at momma and she looked right back at me.

"The red ball; that is all," she said.

"No, no, no," I shrieked, stomping my feet and turning as red as the ball and drum set. "I want those toys. I want more toys; I want….."

Momma grabbed me by my sundress straps and guided me quickly outside, waving to her sister to follow. We stood on the sidewalk in front of the toys displayed in the window as momma proceeded to inform me that as of now, it was no toys at all. No red ball, no red drums; nothing. I howled in indignant protest but my objections fell on deaf ears. We were going home.

The bus pulled up and my aunt, momma and I boarded, finding three seats together near the front. The door slammed shut and the bus chugged forth, black puffs of exhaust smoke billowing out behind it. I slumped in the corner of my seat, head resting on the dirty window, muttering under my breath, "A toy; I want a toy; I want a toy…." Momma and her sister were engrossed in a lively conversation, pointedly ignoring me, avoiding me, pretending not to hear me. "A toy; I want a toy; a toy; a toy…." and the litany went on and on for the entire twenty minutes of the trip home.

As we neared our stop, my aunt pulled the buzzer to signal the driver. The bus came to a halt, shuddering and wheezing and the three of us descended. As soon as my feet touched the ground, I crumbled in a heap on the dusty road. I was huddled near the huge front wheels of the bus, my little body writhing in pain. Momma let out a scream. The bus driver jumped out of the bus to join momma and my aunt as they knelt down beside me, gently touching me, afraid to cause further injuries.

"Oh, my God," momma moaned, "the bus must have hit her!" She looked anxiously around her, searching for anyone that could come help move me. She leaned down close to me, caressing my face and asked me how I was. Where did I hurt? Could I tell her what had happened?

I turned over slightly, looked up at her with tear-filled eyes and whimpered, "You didn't buy me a toy!"

Toys R-4-Me!

THE GIFT

The house was quiet. Everyone was napping. As usual, I was not. In my five-year-old estimation, a country where everyone napped every afternoon was not for me.

The shutters were tightly shut to block out the blistering sun. The patio awning was down. Silence prevailed. I jumped from my bed and tiptoed across the room to where momma was sleeping. She looked serene and free of stress. Her eyes were shut and small even breaths indicated she was in a deep sleep. I was safe.

I opened the bedroom door a crack and quickly made my exit. I walked down the long hallway and into the kitchen. The icebox beckoned. I opened the door to see what I could feast on. A large block of ice purchased that morning was slowly melting as it cooled the contents. A clay pitcher of milk, a bowl of fruit and a platter of cheese took up the top shelf. Meat wrapped in parchment paper took up the second shelf and a variety of fruits and vegetables were scattered on the bottom shelf. I helped myself to fresh figs and an apple and wandered out to the patio. The black and white tiles were hot and my feet burned as I skipped from one tile to another. I squatted under the fig tree and relished the shade it offered me. I feasted greedily as I sat in the stillness of the afternoon.

Quiet enveloped the patio as the afternoon siesta continued. Shade from surrounding bushes and trees cooled the perimeter of the patio. I wiped my hands on my pajamas, staining them with fruit juices, as I contemplated my next adventure. Walking along the edge of the patio, stepping from one shaded block to another, I made my way to the front of the house and to the door of the guest bedroom.

Aunt Athena had recently announced her engagement and the guest bedroom was beginning to fill with gifts. The dowry trunk was open. It was full to the very top with hand-embroidered sheets, pillowcases and towels. Dainty lingerie and robes, all made by Aunt Athena, filled the many drawers of the steamer trunk. I was intrigued and touched each and every item. The bed was covered with a beautiful white crocheted spread. I had heard my grandmother telling momma how many months it had taken to finish it. It was so beautiful and I caressed each square, fluffing the flower centered in each square.

A pen and a piece of paper had been left on a nearby table and I decided to draw something to pass the time. I placed the paper on one of the crocheted squares and began to trace the design. With lips pursed in deep concentration I followed the pattern, pleased with my creation as it emerged. Suddenly, a door slammed. The noise frightened me and the pen slipped off of the paper. A long black squiggle landed on the pristine white of the bedspread. I was scared. I had defaced my aunt's bridal bedspread. What to do? I licked one finger and proceeded to erase the mark. Momma always used that method to clean my chin of various dirt spots; surely, it would clean the ink mark. The mark, however, grew larger and darker. I had to find a way to cover it before anyone discovered it.

I raced back to the bedroom where momma was still sleeping, lost in pleasant dreams. I snatched my favorite Shirley Temple doll and scampered back to the guestroom. I settled the doll on the bed and fluffed the pink organdy ruffles of her dress over the ink stain. I smoothed her hair into blonde ringlets and kissed her gently before I left the room. I closed the door quietly and went back to my bed to finish my siesta.

As afternoon coffee and cookies were being served for the after-siesta meal, I sat next to Aunt Athena. I touched her engagement ring and admired the solitary diamond as it glittered and sparkled. I sighed and looked at Aunt Athena with dark, sad eyes.

"Aunt Athena," I began, "we won't be here for your wedding; we'll be home in America." I sighed forlornly. "But I love you so much, I gave you a wedding present today."

"Ahhh, what a sweet little girl you are," murmured Aunt Athena. "What did you give me?"

"My Shirley Temple doll. I want you to remember me for ever and ever. I put it on your bride's bed. Don't move it until it is time to use the bed. Just remember me, okay?"

Aunt Athena looked at momma as tears welled up in her eyes. "Maria, what a sweet girl you have. How thoughtful to sacrifice her favorite doll. She isn't as bad as we've thought all these months. She really is a very caring child." She turned to me and said, "Thank you, Stella. I'll cherish that doll until I have a little girl of my own to give it to."

I grimaced at the thought of another little girl taking possession of my Shirley. I had paid dearly for my misdeed today, truly I had. I left the table forlornly and went in search of another doll. Shirley had been sacrificed and I would never forget her.

the doll I left behind

my aunt (and her husband)… – recipient of my doll!

COMFORT ZONE

I was finally getting used to being in Greece. I became accustomed to the mandatory afternoon naps. I liked the snacks served after naptime. I liked having dinner late outside on the patio or at a nearby sidewalk restaurant. I liked being able to stay up later than I had ever been allowed to do back home. The midday heat didn't seem as oppressive anymore and the rocky beaches didn't hurt my feet as much now. I liked to stand in the ocean and gaze through the crystal clear water at the multi-colored pebbles on the ocean floor. I had already gathered a vast collection of pebbles and rocks to take back to America. I was getting used to this strange country - but I still cried.

One day, momma came into the bedroom and shook me awake. "Get up, Stella; it's almost 9 o'clock."

"So?" I asked as I rolled over and nestled into the soft cotton blanket.

"We're going into Athens and you are coming with us."

I rolled over at gazed at the ceiling. "What for?"

I had been banned from shopping excursions and now I was being invited on one? Why?

"We have a surprise for you. Come on, get up."

Not one to overlook a surprise, I jumped off the bed and onto the cool marble floor. I threw on a sundress and stepped into my sandals. I was ready.

Momma made me go back and wash my face, brush my teeth, comb my hair and change my underwear. I had to have breakfast. I had to wait for momma and her sister to get ready. Then and only then could we take the trip into Athens, my "forbidden city." But for what, I still did not know.

The bus chugged and sputtered its way into the city. I did my best to sit still and not whine. I wanted to be worthy of my surprise. Momma and her sister chatted, oblivious to my silence.

The city was by now stifling hot. Heat waves shimmered upwards from the streets. Awnings were pulled down, shading shop windows like droopy eyelids. People scurried from shop to shop, trying to finish their many errands. Shops, markets, restaurants closed at mid-day. They would reopen in the late afternoon after the sun had lost some of its intensity. There was no time to waste.

We passed the toy store and I slowed my pace. Momma jerked me along, memories of the last visit there all too vivid and not worthy of repeating. I said nothing.

We turned at the next corner and momma began looking at the numbers on the buildings. She stopped before a small shop. It didn't look at all interesting to me, so why were we stopping? A window display consisted of bolts of fabric and not much more. Momma opened the door and she and her sister entered. I stood on the sidewalk and gazed at the boring window display and wondered what was inside that would interest me?

Momma came back out and guided me into the shop. We walked towards the back where my aunt was waiting for us. She was smiling as if she had a secret too big to contain. What was going on here?

"Ahhhh, good morning, Mesdames," the shopowner murmured. "And good morning to you, Mademoiselle," he said as he gazed at me. "A petite mademoiselle, very charming. Beautiful eyes," he stated as he continued leering at me.

I did not like this. I glared back at him and plopped into a nearby chair.

Momma walked up closer to the counter. She and the shopwner were in deep conversation. She pulled a piece of paper from her purse and handed it to him. He smiled and walked to the back of the store and through a closed door.

Momma and her sister pulled up two chairs and sat down next to me. The air was still and the room was dim. A fly buzzed somewhere, its droning breaking the quiet. I was determined to be good but this was not my type of store and I couldn't envision what the surprise could possibly be.

A young girl approached us with a tray. She offered us tall glasses of cool water. She gave us each a small glass dish holding a miniature silver spoon filled with homemade cherry preserves. I perked up. This was my most favorite treat. A traditional offering to guests in homes and businesses alike, a tradition that really appealed to me.

I grasped one of the glasses, cold to the touch. Beads of moisture trickled down the smooth glass. I carefully immersed the spoonful of cherry preserves into the water. I swirled and twirled the silver spoon, the preserves soon tinting the water a deep red. The cherries settled to the bottom of the glass. The best way to enjoy this delight, I had learned, was to drink the liquid first and then slowly savor the sweet, plump cherries that nestled on the bottom.

I lifted the glass to my parched lips and let the cold sweet nectar trickle down my throat. I sipped slowly, not wanting the moment to end. I sipped some more, quietly emptying the glass. All that was left now were the cherries on the bottom of the glass. Not nearly as many as I would have liked, but I did not express my dissatisfaction. I lowered the spoon into the glass, capturing a few cherries, and brought them to my mouth. I quickly devoured them and returned the spoon to the glass, scraping the bottom for the last of the sweet, ruby red cherries.

The empty glasses were placed on the tray and momma, her sister and I settled back in our chairs to wait for the shopowner.

I heard a rustling noise and looked up to see him emerging through the door, a large bundle cradled in his arms. It was wrapped in brown paper and tied tightly with twine. "Ahhh, Madame, sorry for the delay. Here it is," he said as he beckoned momma to come towards the counter.

Momma and her sister stepped up to the counter. I remained in my chair. Momma quickly ripped the paper and snipped the twine away. "Here, Stella, come see what we have here. It is for you."

I frowned as I looked at the bulky package on the counter. I jumped down from the chair and walked towards momma, sandals slapping the hard concrete floor. "What is it?" I asked; "What's for me?"

Momma discarded the brown wrapping paper and twine. There on the counter was the most beautiful quilted comforter I had ever seen. It was a deep rose, with a twirling quilted stitching all over it. I touched it. It was so soft. I lifted one corner and to my amazement the reverse side was a deep burgundy with a scroll pattern in an amber shade. It was beautiful and I stared at it in speechless wonder.

Momma and her sister exchanged glances and smiles as they witnessed my joy. I turned to momma and in a quivery voice asked, "Is this really for me? Me?"

"Yes," momma answered. "It was made especially for you. You now have your very own comforter for your naps here and for your bed when we go back home to America. Do you like it?"

"Oh, yes, oh, yes!" I squealed, caressing the soft folds of my very own comforter. I couldn't wait to take a nap. I couldn't wait to put it on the marble floor and rest on it. I couldn't wait for winter so I could snuggle under it. I never, ever imagined having my own comforter!

The shopowner laughed heartily at my joy. "Do you think you can carry it?" he asked me.

"I can, I can!" I replied.

He tied twine around it, encircling it several times and placed a little wooden handle on the twine. He gave it to me and I grabbed the handle and started off towards the door.

"Come on, momma; come on; it's almost naptime!"

Everyone laughed as I staggered through the door. I refused to give up the bundle. It was not heavy, just cumbersome, but I wanted no help.

We boarded the bus and I sat apart from momma and my aunt, sharing a seat only with my comforter. We descended the bus and I ran towards my grandmother's house, my sandaled feet racing homeward. I passed the little goat tethered at the gate and gleefully told it I had a new comforter. I banged the iron gates open and ran down the black and white tiles of the patio, calling out for my grandmother.

"Look, look," I shouted. "My own comforter for my naps. Is it naptime yet?"

"Yes, yes," said my grandmother as she looked heavenward and made the sign of the cross.

Peace had finally come to the household.

RED SANDALS

No more shopping trips for me, momma had warned. However, my daily pleadings for toys and surprises did not cease. Momma and her sister continued their weekly shopping trips, but without me. I waited at home for new toys to be brought to me.

Momma's most recent surprise for me was not a toy, much to my disappointment. I had unwrapped the package eagerly only to find a pair of red sandals….red leather criss-crossed straps and shiny wooden soles. Everyone wore them to the beach and I had secretly coveted them. And now, they were mine. I quickly slid them on my feet, wiggling my toes down to the tips to ensure a good fit. I stomped one foot and then the other. They fit, they made noise and I would no longer have to wear socks and shoes from America.

I wore the sandals everywhere. If I could have slept with them by my side, I would have. I clomped and stomped up and down the patio every day, all day. Clomp; clomp; clomp;! I couldn't wait to get back to America and show my friends my beautiful red sandals.

Much to momma's consternation, the sandals soon became a total nuisance and annoyance. The daily clomping did not cease. Naptimes were disrupted by my jumping and running, the noise becoming more irritating as I became more adept in my gymnastics. The patio tiles resounded daily with the clatter of my wooden soles.

Something had to be done. Momma hid the sandals one day but the turmoil generated by their loss soon brought forth the sandals from their hiding place. I continued to clomp and stomp as momma cursed the day she had bought the sandals. I was the envy of my cousins and the dread of momma, grandmother and aunt. Momma realized one day that the shiny red sandals had brought an end to my daily crying. Surely, the clomping was preferable to the crying. And so, she made peace with herself.

I soon tired of the novelty and the sandals were kicked aside. Crying commenced once again, lamenting my distance from daddy, toys and friends. Thoughts churned in my head as to what new toys and surprises would emerge from this new outbreak of tears.

Between tears, I ran barefooted on the tile patio and barefooted on the dusty sidewalk and barefooted on the beach. The little red sandals were long forgotten but the freedom they had provided me kept me from returning to the confines of socks and my American Mary Janes.

Soon, it was time to pack the sandals, my toys and clothes, for we were going back to America. The crying ceased as I eagerly searched every room to be sure we were not forgetting anything. I shook my finger at my aunt and reminded her that if anything, anything at all, was left behind, she was to be sure to mail it to us right away.

Suddenly, I was a cheerful child, a funny child, a loving child. We were going back to America, to daddy, to my toys and to my friends. I was now a happy child.

my favorite uncle, Stefanos

TRANSFORMATION

The six-month stay in Greece was finally coming to an end. The miserable (in my estimation) months had passed all too slowly but soon momma and I would be going home.

Despite my constant whining, crying and troublemaking, I had been pampered and spoiled. I was the youngest of the grandchildren. I was a novelty, the American relative. I was placed on a pedestal from which I constantly fell.

Shopping trips had been placed off-limits due to my excessive demands, but entertainment had been provided daily. I was allowed to play in the tiled patio every day. Cousins were recruited to take me to the beach for hours of splashing in the crystal clear ocean. An occasional movie, puppet show or trip to the local pastry shop were all special treats.

Momma had long passed the "end of her rope" with me. She pleaded with me. She promised treats. She spanked and pinched me. She sought refuge in her room. She threatened to disown me. She prayed to God for deliverance from this wicked child. All to no avail. I had been a terror.

It was now August and two weeks remained before we were to set sail for America. Momma was slowly packing our clothes and picking up stray toys. I followed her everywhere to ensure that nothing of our was left behind. I looked under beds and on top of closets. I left strict orders that anything we left behind was to be mailed to us immediately. I was the inventory taker and nothing would be forgotten.

This day promised to be a hot and sticky one just like so many before. There was no breeze anywhere. I sat in wilted disarray on the marble steps, plotting my plan for the day. Momma came out into the breezeway and sat down beside me. She hugged me and wiped beads of perspiration from my flushed face. She brushed my bangs, pinning them back with a bobby pin. She smiled. I frowned. I began to cry.

"Stop that. We're going on a trip today."

I stared ahead. "Where? Why?"

"Because," she replied. "Now, get up and put on a clean dress. We're going to Dinos."

"Why?" I whined. "I don't want to. I hate Dinos."

"You've never been there,"momma informed. "Now, get up. Now!"

I knew better than to push the issue any further. I got up and trudged back towards the bedroom to search for a clean, cool dress. I banged the door open into the bedroom and slammed it shut. I really didn't want to go.

"Hurry up," momma shouted. "The taxi will be here soon."

Taxi? A taxi? My spirits soared. A clean dress was quickly found and tossed onto my sweaty body. Bare feet were forced into sandals and a quick swipe of a comb arranged my bedraggled, sweaty, tangled hair. I was ready.

Momma stood waiting in the patio, a suitcase beside her. My grandmother and aunt stood near her along with a myriad of suitcases and baskets of food. The taxi arrived and we were on the way.

The taxi chugged its way down towards the docks and to a waiting ferry boat. The fare was paid, suitcases and baskets retrieved and we made our clumsy way to the platform marked "Dinos." We climbed the swaying steps onto the shiny deck of the boat. Whistles blasted, sailor shouted, people laughed and cheered as the boat slowly slid out of the harbor. We were going to Dinos.

"What's Dinos, momma?" I asked, tugging at her skirt as it billowed out in the breeze. “What can I do there?”

“You’ll see,” momma answered as she turned to face the salt spray blowing up from the churning waves. “Ahhhhh, this is so nice, so cool; ahhhhh…” and she continued to lean into the ocean spray.

The ferry made its way across the watery path and soon came to the island of Dinos. Colorful banners and flags fluttered in the breeze. The blazing sun bounced off of the white-washed houses, blinding us. Throngs of people waited at the edge of the dock for the boat to pull safely into the harbor. A throbbing source of energy poured over us. The excitement was intense.

We flagged a passing taxi and once settled, momma directed the driver to take us to the “monasteri.” I reviewed my limited Greek vocabulary and could not find “monasteri.” I tugged at momma’s arm as I asked, “Where are we going, momma?

“You’ll see; we’ll be there soon.”

I wiggled further back onto the dilapidated seat of the taxi and wondered where I was being taken and why. I started to cry.

“Look, look,” momma whispered, “look.”

I stared out of the open taxi window and saw a huge church with many ornate domes looming ahead. It was pristine white and seemed to shimmer in the heat of the day. Curving staircases led to the upper balconies and arched marble pillars supported the vastness of it. We jumped out of the taxi and joined the crowds milling around us. We were jostled, bumped into, pushed against and pulled as we made our way towards the church. I grasped momma’s belt and held on tightly as we made our way through the throngs of humanity. The noise was pulsating. The aroma of food being offered by street vendors was intoxicating. The excitement of the crowd overpowered us and swept us away with it.

We reached the staircase leading to the massive front door of the church. Momma helped me climb the steps as they were very steep and slippery. I held on to her hand as she tugged me up the steps, one by one, until we reached the top, with my grandmother and aunt following. The massive door confronted us. A huge brass door knocker was centered on the door and momma banged it until the door was slowly opened. A wrinkled, weathered face peered out at us, framed by a white scarf, the body enveloped in voluminous black robes. Momma stepped closer and a conversation ensued. Money was placed into the outstretched, scrawny hands and a slip of paper was placed in momma's hands in exchange. The door creaked closed.

"Come on, come on," momma shouted as she led the way down the stairs. At the bottom, she stopped and glanced at the paper she held in her hands. "This way," she said, as we followed her through an archway and down a short corridor. She stopped before a battered and weather-beaten wooden door bearing the number 5. "This is ours; let's go in."

"No!" I screamed. "I'm not going into a dungeon!" I planted my feet firmly and dared anyone to force me into that room. "NO!" I shouted again.

Momma quickly yanked my arm and propelled me inside, followed by my aunt and grandmother, slamming the door closed behind her. The room was small and sparse. Candles flickered from niches in the walls. Four cots had been set up, covered with freshly washed and ironed cotton sheets. A thin, well-worn gray blanket was folded at the foot of each cot to ward off any unforeseen chills. A few rickety chairs and a worn washstand were the only other furnishings. I gazed in bewilderment at the sparse and sadly neglected room.

My aunt and grandmother soon busied themselves removing food from the baskets and pushing suitcases under the cots. A hand-woven blanket was spread out on the floor. They sat on the blanket and began to sort out the food. "A picnic," I thought. "Why didn't momma tell me? A picnic! What fun!"

I was starving. My early breakfast of cocoa and bread had long been digested. “I’m ready to eat,” I announced as I plopped down on the blanketed floor.

Eggs, bread, butter, cheese, olives, onions, tomatoes, cucumbers and a variety of fruit were passed around. Wine was poured. It was a feast worthy of the ancient gods. I grabbed bread and tomatoes and began to devour them. Olives were licked, chewed and pits spit out. Hard-boiled eggs were placed in n a bowl and passed around. Hungry hands grabbed their share and the eerie silence of the room was broken by the sound of eggs being cracked open. I selected the largest egg I could find and began to hit it on the side of the bowl. I was n a hurry to crack it open, peel it and savor the yolk, my favorite part.

I hit the egg against the rim of the bowl again and again. Nothing happened. One more time, much harder. Again, nothing, not even a crack.

“Ehhhhh,” momma screeched. “Ehhhhhh!”

She snatched the egg from my hands as I sat in stunned silence, mouth wide open waiting to devour my egg.

I started to cry. I cried from hunger and bewilderment. Tears poured and my cries became hysterical.

“For the name of God,” shouted my aunt. “What are you doing to her, Maria? The child wants to eat, she’s hungry.”

“I forgot. We all forgot,” momma said. “We came here for her to take communion and be blessed by the Holy Virgin Mary of Dinos. She can’t have milk or cheese or eggs. Remember? She has to fast for communion tomorrow morning.”

With that, momma hit my egg against the side of the bowl. Once, twice; nothing. She smashed it against the hard dirt floor and on the third try, the shell cracked. Momma peeled away the alabaster egg shell to reveal a hardened, petrified amber yolk.

Hands went up and down in unison making the sign of the cross. My grandmother whispered prayers in a monotone. My aunt knelt and kissed the ground we were sitting on. Momma cuddled and kissed me over and over.

"We just had a miracle here. The Virgin Mary gave you a miracle, Stella. She wanted you to take communion tomorrow even though we forgot. A true miracle."

My eyes and mouth opened wide in utter amazement.

I looked at the amber rock that was to have been my dinner. I touched it and it was cold and hard. I looked at the eggs the others had peeled. They were all ordinary hard-boiled eggs. I was being told by God not to eat the egg. I was being told to prepare myself for communion. I was meant to receive communion and be blessed. I was stunned and silent.

I snatched more bread and another tomato. I quickly crossed myself and silently thanked God for my special miracle.

I became a transformed child.

Momma, Yaya and me – in front of the church on Dinos Island

And so, the Grecian Odyssey ended. My mother and I returned home, she to a hoped-for improved marriage and I to my daddy, my toys and my friends. I now spoke only Greek, my limited English having long been forgotten. I returned as a happy, suntanned little girl, no longer whining and crying for I was home again.

THE DRESS

Though the long visit to Greece had come to an end and I was back home with daddy, toys and friends, Momma was sad as she remembered leaving her mother, sister and brothers once again, not knowing if she would ever see them again. She was reliving her separation from them all over again.

I, on the other hand, entertained my little friends daily with stories of my Grecian adventures, tending to exaggerate at times. I liked impressing them with my flawless Greek. We all spoke Greek at home and among ourselves as we had limited exposure to anyone outside of our Greek neighborhood. We lived in the "Greek Ghetto" and happy in our ignorance. The Greek we spoke was not the same as that which I had recently learned in Greece. I learned formal Greek and the proper names for objects rather than the "Americanized" versions we used at home. For instance, "bisikla" was what I called my bike at home, but in Greece the proper noun was "pothilato." "Tsunga" was chewing gun at home, and "mastihi" in Greece. So, I was now a learned scholar of the Greek language and eager to impress one and all. My friends soon hated me.

It was now a warm Sunday, an Indian summer kind of day. Momma, daddy and I enjoyed a leisurely breakfast as we made plans for the day. It was decided we would take a drive out to the park and then stop to see friends that momma and daddy had not seen for a while.

Momma cleared the table, washed and dried the dishes and put them away. She swept the kitchen floor, checked the refrigerator's ("ice-boxey") contents to plan dinner for that evening and got out the pots and pans she would need. Once she was satisfied that all was in order, she ascended the stairs to my bedroom to help me get dressed for the day's outing.

"Here, Stella," she said. "You can wear this today," and she placed the dress on my bed. I took one look and knew a battle was about to begin.

"No," I said. "I don't like it."

It was a dress momma had brought back from Greece. It was handmade and hand-embroidered. It had smocking across the shoulders and fell in soft folds straight down from the shoulders. It was made of soft white cotton, flimsy as fairy wings. The smocking and embroidery were done in a soft blue. I hated it because it was too "babyish." It had no waist and no one else among my neighborhood friends had ever worn anything like it. I was not going to wear it.

Momma was determined that I was to wear the beautiful dress from Greece. It had been made by my mother's sister and held much love within each stitch. I shook my head at momma. I perched on the edge of the bed, arms crossed and legs swinging in defiance. She came at me, waving the dress and warning me not to cross her.

I ran out of the bedroom with momma in hot pursuit. I ran into the living room in a frantic search for daddy. He wasn't there. I stood frozen in fright, knowing momma was just a few steps from grabbing me. I saw that the living room bay window was wide open in an effort to let some air into the house. It was an unusually warm day and although the screens had been taken down in preparation for winter, the window had been raised to offer some relief from the unexpected heat. I separated the sheer curtains and jumped over the windowsill, landing on the front porch. There was daddy sitting in the rocking chair, waiting for us to begin the Sunday drive.

I quickly jumped onto his lap, crumbling the newspaper he had been reading, and hugged him tightly around his neck, burrowing my face into his white-shirted chest. I began to cry.

"What is wrong with you?" he asked. "Why aren't you dressed?" There I was, in undershirt and panties and nothing more.

"'Cause I don't like my dress," I stated. "I hate it and won't wear it." I burrowed deeper as his arms encircled me and I felt the warmth of his protection surrounding me. I was safe now.

Momma rushed out onto the porch, hated dress in hand. “Chris, do something!” she pleaded. “Stella is being a monster and I won’t have it. She can’t spoil today for us. She has to get dressed so we can leave.”

She threw the dress at me and stomped off. Daddy picked up the dress and began to examine it. “Mmmmmm,” he murmured, “this is a very pretty and unusual dress. I think it needs a very pretty little girl to wear it and do it justice.”

I blinked back my tears and looked up at him. I couldn’t believe what I was hearing.

“Yes, yes,” he continued, “this is a very spectacular dress. No one else in America has a dress this beautiful. Only Stella has this dress; only Stella can wear it and only Stella can do it justice.”

I smiled smugly, agreeing with my daddy. I picked up the dress and examined it closely. It was so soft and sheer and the blue embroidered design was quite unusual. Maybe I should wear it. If daddy said I should, then I would.

“Do you think I should wear this, daddy? Will I look funny? Don’t you think it is ugly and old-fashioned?”

“No, no, I don’t think that at all,” he assured me. “It is a very special dress made for a very special little girl. I think you should wear it and let everyone see it.”

I jumped off his lap. Daddy helped me pull the dress over my head and guided the soft folds as they careened down my sturdy chest and protruding tummy. I fluffed the tiny puffed sleeves and smoothed the smocking across my chest and shoulders. Daddy looked at me and a slow grin appeared on his face. “Very nice, Stella, very nice. You look pretty and the dress is beautiful. No one has a dress like this one.” He kissed me on the cheek, patted me on my backside and gently guided me through the front door back into the living room.

"Momma," I yelled. "I'm ready. Where are my shoes? Let's go." I was eager to show off my finery.

"Maria," called daddy, "where are you? What's taking you so long; let's go."

And so, another Sunday drive began.

I started school not long after the return from Greece. I spoke no English but nothing daunted me. Although I didn't want to leave home and all of its pleasures, I wanted to experience being a "school girl." I conquered the obstacles and became a "teacher's delight"…..a terror at home but an angel at school, for some strange reason.

SCHOOL DAZE

Reluctant as I was to leave home, the anticipation of a world waiting to be discovered lured me, and so, I decided I would go to school.

Momma buttoned up my sweater, secured the bows in my braids and put a clean handkerchief in my pocket. New pencils and notebooks were clutched tightly in my hands as I walked to the door. I looked back at her with a forlorn gaze but she quickly waved me on. I was six now, a big girl, off to first grade.

Kally, Lula and Mary waited impatiently outside for me, anxious to go. They were all a year ahead of me, already acquainted with the school route and school schedules. They were ready to pass on their words of wisdom to me. I opened the door and slowly inched my way out onto the front porch.

Although the excitement of new experiences was tempting, home, with its familiar sounds and its sameness of routine, was a security I wasn't eager to give up. I wouldn't be home when Kally's momma visited. I wouldn't hear the latest gossip. I wouldn't know if Mrs. Pete had returned the handkerchief she had borrowed from momma. I wouldn't see daddy when he came home from work. I wouldn't be able to sleep till ten. I wouldn't be able to stay up late. I wouldn't be free any more. Daddy had said I didn't have to go to school so why wouldn't momma listen to him? Just the other day I had whispered to him that I had a very bad cold, demonstrating its severity by blowing hard into my handkerchief. "Oh, yes," he had exclaimed; "you are one sick child. Maria, Stella has a cold; we'll keep her home!" My eyes sparkled and I blew even harder. Momma never even acknowledged daddy's command. She didn't believe either one of us; the father/daughter conspiracy had failed.

Off to school it was. Kally, Lula and Mary guided the way and I soon entered the hallowed hallways of P.S. #5. Other first-graders were already in place and I took the nearest empty desk. I placed the pencils and tablets on top and waited to see what would happen next. The teacher entered the room, a commanding presence. I pulled my socks up, smoothed out the pleats of my new skirt, sat up a little straighter and folded my hands, just as Kally, Lula and Mary had told me to do.

The hours passed in a blur of activities. I was overwhelmed, fascinated by it all, forgetting the hesitancy of my morning. This was not at all frightening or intimidating. It was exciting; I was learning so many new things. I couldn't wait to tell my friends; I couldn't wait to report to momma and daddy.

Three o'clock came all too soon. The bell clanged, terminating my first day of school. I picked up my pencils and tablet and waited outside for my friends to collect me for the walk back home. I saw them coming towards me and I jumped up and down, waving, making sure they saw me. The four of us started the short walk back, anticipating the milk and cookies waiting for us. We marched in unison, left, right, left....we were comrades, pals, friends...and scholars.

I roared into the house, my braids undone, sweater unbuttoned, wildly waving my artistic accomplishments of the day. "Look; look what I did today!" I screamed. Momma stooped down and caught me in a hug, almost falling over with the intensity of my flight.

"Oh, how pretty!", she said, gallantly trying to decipher the whorls of color on the papers scattered about her. "We'll show daddy when he comes home; won't he be surprised?" I proudly gathered my artwork, placing it carefully between the pages of my tablet, saving it for a second showing when daddy got home, protecting it for the second day of school.

I had lost most of my limited English vocabulary while in Greece and momma was concerned. How would I understand instructions? How would I make new friends? How would I ask questions? How overwhelming the day must have been for me. "Stella," momma began, "how was your first day? What did you do? Did you understand the teacher?" Her concern was great.

"No, momma," I whispered; "I just pretend."

HAGERSTOWN, MARYLAND
1938 - 1949

First grade in Reading, Pennsylvania was over. My father was now the proprietor of a restaurant and the summer before second grade found us in Hagerstown. Maryland. We knew no one there. There was no Greek community other than a few old bachelors and one family with grown children. To top it all off, my father knew nothing about the restaurant business. He tackled the opportunity by the "seat of his pants" and the "sweat of his brow" and went on to make the "Plaza Restaurant" one of the better restaurants in town. People still remember the Plaza at 18 North Potomac Street.

BIRDS OF A FEATHER.....

We moved into an apartment near the restaurant my daddy had bought in Hagerstown, Maryland. I liked our apartment. It was on the top floor of an big, old house. We had a large kitchen, living room, two bedrooms and a bathroom with a huge bathtub. Mrs. Stevens, the landlady, scared me just a little bit. She was tiny, old and wrinkled. But she had a parrot…a brightly colored green and yellow parrot with a big black beak. It shrieked and chattered and carried on imaginary conversations all day. I would wait anxiously for Mrs. Stevens to invite me into her apartment downstairs. I would tiptoe over to the parrot's cage. I would cautiously put out my hand to touch the green and yellow feathers, and shrieked as it jabbed me with its beak. It was a challenge each time to snatch my hand away, fingers still intact.

Our new apartment soon felt like home and momma was busy making it as comfortable as could be. Daddy was busy with the restaurant School would start in September, three months away, and I would face second grade and its challenges. But now, summer and freedom were mine. There were no other children in the apartment house and I had yet to spot any in the neighborhood. I was lonely and missed my friends from Reed Street in Reading, Pennsylvania. Momma played with me whenever she could and daddy would ask me how my day went when he would finally came home from the restaurant. That was all very nice but I needed friends.

Days went by and I became familiar with the house and the big yard around it. I soon felt it was time to venture beyond my current boundaries. One day I took a big breath - for strength and courage - and opened the garden gate. I looked up and down the street and saw no one. A dog suddenly came scampering down the street, straight for me. I retreated back into the security of the backyard. I heard someone laughing and peeked over the fence. A little girl was looking back at me and we stared at each other. She smiled first; I was more cautious. "Hi,", she said, her blue eyes sparkling. I replied "Hi," shyly smiling back at her. Silence followed. "He won't hurt," she knowingly advised me. "It's just the dog from across the street….Sparky. He's gone now." I stood on tip-toes looking over the picket fence to assure myself that Sparky was truly out of sight. He was. I opened the gate and stepped out as I was determined to discover what was beyond the picket fence. She came up to me and said, "My name is Sharon; what's yours?"

"Stella," I said and stopped. I didn't know what else to say. I had never had to make new friends before. She took me by the hand and pulled me along to the side of the house. There in the dug-up dirt was a treasure trove of toys, and they were all hers! This had possibilities of a friendship, I thought.

We played, we laughed and cautiously learned about each other. She, too, would be starting second grade in September. We promised we would walk to school together for the first day and every day after that. She was blonde and fair, with big blue eyes. I, with my black hair, olive skin and dark eyes stood in sharp contrast next to her. Her effervescence overshadowed my reticence and somehow we brought out the best in each other. We were friends.

Most of my toys were still packed away and I didn't have much to share as yet. But the parrot in Mrs. Stevens living room was something way beyond toys. I took Sharon's hand and guided her into the yard, up the front porch steps and into Mrs. Stevens' living room. The parrot perched on its birdcage swing in all its feathery splendor. It sputtered and stuttered its full range of vocabulary. Sharon's eyes grew wide in amazement. She had never seen anything like this before! With my great wisdom I warned her not to dare touch the parrot; only I was allowed to do that. I approached the parrot with a great show of bravado. I tentatively stroked the green and yellow feathers, silently praying my fingers would be left intact. Sharon stared in awe as I grinned with pride.

We left the parrot shrieking and muttering in its cage and we skipped outside once again, to plan and plot the days ahead. Joy was all mine, for I had a friend.

MY NAME IS.....

We moved again mid-way through second grade. We were in a house once again after living in an apartment. I would miss the few friends I had made at Broadway Elementary. I would miss Sharon, my best friend. I would miss our landlord's green and yellow parrot. But, I would not miss the apartment too much as I now had a three-story house at 206 East Franklin Street and a new neighborhood to explore.

Antietam Elementary was three blocks away. I had to start midway through second grade, had to make new friends and learn names of new teachers. I knew no one at Antietam Elementary. I remember walking into classroom 2-A and immediately felt as if a spotlight had turned on me. The already seated students gazed at me as I walked towards the back. I headed for an empty desk, hoping to blend into the background. I sat primly, folding my hands in front of me as I had learned back in first grade. I waited. The other girls and boys continued to stare. I felt out of place. I was the only one with coal black hair and dark eyes. Everyone else was either blonde and blue-eyed or had light brown hair with brown or hazel eyes. I sensed I was different. I lowered my eyes, avoiding the scrutiny I was obviously under.

The teacher cleared her throat and stood up from her desk. She introduced herself as Mrs. Shue. "It is spelled S-h-u-e, not s-h-o-e, but pronounced the same. Mrs. Shue." She smiled at the eager faces before her.

"Now," she said, let's get our desk assignments. I want everyone to sit in alphabetical order to that I may learn your names faster and know what desk you are assigned. We'll begin with names starting with A." She proceeded to rearrange the class amidst the ensuing confusion.

I settled into my new desk and quickly made it mine. I placed pencils in the groove at the top of the desk and stored books and book satchel on the shelf under the desk chair. I looked at the students sitting at desks in front of me, beside me and in back of me.

"Now, then," Mrs. Shue announced. "I want each of you to stand, one by one and introduce yourself. Give your first name only for now; that way, we can get acquainted faster."

That done, I had high hopes that my classmates and I would soon become friends. The boy in back of me smiled and I felt better. He had blond hair and big brown eyes. He seemed quiet and shy. I liked him. I remembered his name - Stanley - and hoped he would soon talk to me. I shifted my bottom on the hard desk seat until I found the most comfortable spot and waited for the lessons to begin.

Days went by. I loved learning new things and felt challenged to earn gold stars in spelling and arithmetic I made friends. Joanne was now designated to be best friend. She would take the place of best friend Sharon from Broadway Elementary. I now lived on the other end of town and would probably never see Sharon again. Stanley continued being shy but smiled at me every day. Sometimes we would talk about lessons or check each other's test papers. My first case of puppy love was blossoming slowly but surely.

One Friday afternoon, Joanne invited me to stop by her house for cookies after school. I knew I couldn't stay long as momma expected me home right after school every day. But since Joanne lived only a few houses down from the school, I felt it would be all right to stop in for five minutes. The promise of cookies was too enticing. Off we went, chatting, laughing and bonding in our newfound friendship.

"Hi, mom, I'm home," yelled Joanne as we bounded in through the front door. The smell of freshly baked cookies wafted out from the kitchen to greet us. Joanne and I grinned at each other in great anticipation.

Her mother emerged from the kitchen. "Hello, girls. How was school today?" she asked.

"Fine," we chimed.

"Sit down and have some cookies," she said, and motioned for us to follow her into the kitchen. "I'll get Janie to join us."

Joanne wrinkled her nose. "Janie's my little sister. She's a pain. Ignore her."

Janie entered the kitchen with her mother. She was probably about four years old. She was petite and cute, with dark hair and big brown eyes just like Joanne. She didn't look like very much of a pain to me.

"Mom, Janie," Joanne began, "this is my new friend - my new best friend - Stella." She stopped. "Stella, I don't know your last name. What is it?"

"I'm Stella. Stella Hatgiannis," I said.

"So nice to meet you, Stella," said Joanne's mother. She smiled and offered me more cookies.

"Stella - Stella Hot Pajamas?" chortled Janie.

Joanne was right. Janie was a pain!

****

Now flash forward twenty-five years. I'm at a party. Noise, music, conversations swirl about me.

I'm feeling somewhat adrift, not knowing anyone but eager to meet someone. My girlfriends from work had convinced me to come to this party with them. So there I stood on the sidelines as they danced their way across the floor.

I clutched my drink glass tightly. I forced a smile to convey that I was having a good time - really, I was. I took a sip of the drink. Its liquid fire burned its way down to my belly. It felt good. I took another sip. I smiled and believed I was having a good time - really, I was.

"Hi. Would you like to dance?"

I looked up and saw a young man. Not too young, but definitely younger. Everyone everywhere was younger, it seemed.

"Ummmm, okay," I responded. I took another sip and placed my drink on a nearby table. I put my hand in his and led him to the dance floor.

He smiled down at me and said, "This is my favorite song."

I smiled and said, "Mine, too." Liar, I thought.

We circled the room, slowly swaying to the melodic tune. He hummed in my ear. He pulled me closer.

Oh, God, I thought, what am I doing here?

"Having a good time?" he asked, grinning down at me.

"Oh, yes," I politely replied. He pulled me closer.

"By the way, what's your name?" he ventured to ask.

"Stella - Stella Hatgiannis," I murmured as the music blared around us.

"What?" he asked. "I can't hear you."

"Stella - Stella Hatgiannis," I said. The music swelled around us.

"Stella - Stella Hot Pajamas?" he asked in an incredulous voice. "Hot Pajamas? Hot Damn!"

I was having a good time?

DANCE

We shuffled into the music room, a group of unruly second-graders who wished they were elsewhere. It was a dreary March day, too rainy and miserable to go out for recess and excess energy had to be harnessed somehow.

The music room was large and the floor to ceiling windows looked out upon the bleak and deserted playground. Swings tossed and turned in the blustery wind. Sheets of water slid down the sliding boards, ending in muddy puddles. It was a nasty day but it would not be lost.

"Now, then," instructed Miss Jackson, "we are going to dance." Shrieks, giggles and moans greeted this announcement. Miss Jackson glared at the assembled group, daring it to interrupt her again.

She darted here and there, sorting the group into a large circle, alternating boys and girls as evenly as she could. "Stand still, please. Think of a way to show your feelings to the music. Shall we dance?" Thirty little heads bobbed in unison.

The record was scratchy but the melody was a catchy one. "Express yourself, express yourself," she directed. Bedlam ensued. We were going in every direction, tapping, gliding, jumping - expressing ourselves.

"No, no," screamed Miss Jackson. "This won't do. We'll have to try something else. Back in a circle, please." And we shuffled back into a circle formation.

"I will play a record and one by one you will dance for a few minutes, showing how the music makes you feel. Let's start." The needle fell onto the record and the scratchy sounds of a waltz enveloped the room. "Waltz of the Flowers," Miss Jackson said.

I watched and listened, absorbing the beautiful notes. I had never heard anything like this before. The only music in our house was Greek folk songs and as for dancing, I was not too graceful. In fact, I was a klutz.

I swayed to the music and envisioned myself floating through the air but secretly hoped the class would be over before it was my turn to express myself in dance.

Not to be. "Stella," I heard, "your turn. Let's see what you can do."

Oh, no, I thought; oh, no! What could I do? I stood frozen to the spot.

"Come, come, Stella, into the center of the ring." She pushed me to the rightful spot and pushed the "play" button on the phonograph. Lilting notes came towards me, transporting me to a magic place. I began a slow twirl, arms at my side, feet stumbling.

"Let's see some movement, some feeling," Miss Jackson begged.

I placed my index finger on top of my head, in the very center of my head, and twirled. I was a top, a tilting, twirling top. I spun around and around and around, ending in a heap on the floor.

"Very nice, Stella." She rolled her eyes. "Next, please."

I hated getting up in the morning (still do). I loved staying up at night (still do) and it took all of my mother's repertoire of threats to get me to bed. Getting up was an even greater challenge, with my mother dressing me while I would lie prone under the covers during the process.

SOCK HOP

Time to get up for school and once again, I burrowed deep beneath the covers, escaping reality.

Not that I hated school. I liked school and the whole learning process. I just didn't like getting up so early to start the learning process.

Momma came into my room to begin the usual morning ritual. "Get up, Stella. Get up; you'll be late."

No response.

"NOW!"

I began to stir beneath the mound of blankets. "Not yet, momma; not yet."

Blankets were yanked back and the chill morning air hit me full force. "Get up!" momma said, her voice bordering on hysteria. "Now."

I struggled up to a semi-sitting position, eyes closed in an effort to gain a few more minutes of sweet slumber. I heard momma rummaging through my closet, pulling clothes from hangers and drawers and I knew there was not much sleeping time left.

My pajamas came off and a slip was yanked over my head and settled on my still-prone body. Panties were somehow pulled up over my posterior. I stuck out one leg, and then the other as momma put socks on each foot. A dress was quickly buttoned on. And finally, sturdy school shoes were buckled on my feet. I dozed throughout the entire process.

Momma sat on the edge of the bed to rest. I was lying there, fully clothed and ready for school, but refusing to budge.

She yanked me out of bed on on my feet, shattering my sweet repose. A comb was passed through my tangled hair as I was pushed towards the bathroom to wash my face and brush my teeth. I heard momma sigh in relief as the morning ordeal was over for yet another day.

I emerged from the bathroom, specks of toothpaste still on my face and announced that I wasn't going to school "like that," and pointed towards my feet.

"Why? What's wrong?" momma questioned.

"The socks don't match my dress," I informed her.

"What?" she asked in amazement. "What doesn't match what?"

"My socks," I mumbled. "They don't go with my dress. They're yellow. I have to have white socks."

Momma looked heavenward, uttering a prayer for endurance and patience. "Sit down. I'll find a white pair."

I sat on the bed and yanked shoes and socks off, throwing them helter-skelter as I waited for momma to find the right socks.

"Okay, here we are. White socks."

I wiggled my toes into the socks and stood up to find my shoes. Suddenly, I pulled the socks off and threw them across the room. "No, no. Not silk socks. They're for Sunday dresses." I jumped back on the bed and looked at momma, who was turning purple from rage.

"They're white socks, that's what you wanted and that's what you'll wear! Now, put them on!"

"No," I wailed. "Find another pair of white socks."

Momma dumped the contents of my sock drawer on the bed. She threw socks here, there and everywhere. Blue socks, red socks, yellow socks, pink socks - all went flying through the room. I stared at momma in wide-eyed wonder and questioned her sanity.

"Here, put these on," she said as she flung a pair of white cotton socks towards me. I grabbed them and began to pull them on my very cold feet. I pulled and pulled and pulled until they reached my knees.

"Oh, no! These are knee socks. I won't wear knee socks. I want white short socks." I screamed in agony, pulled off the knee socks and threw myself onto the bed.

Momma shrieked in total frustration. "It's late. You have to put socks on right now and get to school. These are white cotton socks, so put them on!" she demanded.

I wailed and she shrieked and total chaos reigned.

"What's going on up there?" bellowed daddy from the kitchen. "What's happening?"

I dashed out of the bedroom, down the stairs, into the kitchen and jumped onto daddy's lap. He was sipping his morning coffee and reading the paper. He liked quiet in the morning and I could tell he was not in a pleasant mood.

"Daddy, momma wants me to wear ugly socks to school. She doesn't care how I look."

Daddy took a slow sip of coffee and cleared his throat. "Look at me," he said.

I gazed at him through tear-glazed eyes as I awaited his wise decision.

"You do what momma says. Momma picks out your clothes and you wear what she tells you to wear, understand?"

"No!"

My chin trembled as huge tears streamed down my face. This was the first time daddy had failed me. He was on momma's side and I was mortified.

"No!" I screamed again. I jumped down from daddy's lap, ran up the stairs, down the hall and into my bedroom, my sanctuary.

"Stella," warned daddy. "Do what momma says - now!"

"No!" I yelled back as I slammed the bedroom door shut and steeled myself against it, barring any intruders. "No!"

"You do not slam the door shut on me, ever!" boomed daddy as he flung the door wide open, sending me sliding across the polished wood floor. "Put socks on right now!"

Momma stood in the hallway peering at the drama unfolding before her. She was quiet and watchful, a non-participant.

"No," I repeated, with greater defiance.

"No, huh? No, you say?"

Daddy whipped his leather belt off and came towards me. I stood my ground and muttered another "No" as the belt hit my legs. "Whap! Whap!" on one leg and then "Whap! Whap!" on the other.

"Do you understand now?" he asked as he placed the belt back in its rightful place.

I said nothing as he turned and left the room. I gazed at my legs and the criss-crossed red welts that were slowly emerging. Momma said nothing.

"I think I'll wear knee socks today," I muttered as I started pulling on the hated socks.

2 + 3 - 1 =?

"Chris, it's after 4 o'clock and Stella isn't home from school yet. I'm worried."

"Ahhh, you women; always finding something to worry about. She'll be home any minute now," he advised and returned to reading the newspaper.

The clock ticked the minutes away. Momma continued to worry; daddy continued reading the paper.

"Chris, it is now 4:35. Where can she be?" She started to cry.

Daddy sighed, folded the newspaper and pulled himself up and out of the armchair. "I'll go. I'll find her."

He walked the few short blocks to the neighborhood elementary school. Silence enveloped the large brick building. Leaves fluttered to the ground from the majestic trees surrounding the school. The sky was slate gray and the feel of snow was in the air. He looked around and saw no one. He quickly climbed the steps leading to the massive wooden door. He grasped the heavy door handles and pushed the door open. The wooden floor creaked beneath him as he began the search for his small daughter.

The dim overhead lights shed little brilliance as he checked one dark class room after another. Emptiness greeted him in every room. As he turned the far corner he noticed light coming from a door midway down the corridor. He walked swiftly towards the light and yanked the door open, anticipating the worst but hoping for the best.

There I stood before the blackboard. My pigtails had by now come undone, red barrettes long gone. My knee-high socks hung at half-mast. I stood in silence staring at the blackboard in front of me.

Miss Jenkins looked up as she heard the door creak open. "Yes? Who are you, sir? May I help you?"

"Yes, I'm Stella's father. We were worried. I want to take her home."

I turned and stared in astonishment. What was my daddy doing in my classroom? What kind of trouble was I in now?

Miss Jenkins beckoned to him to come in and take a seat. He struggled to fit his massive frame behind the nearest school desk. She motioned for him to be quiet.

"All right, Stella; let's start over again," she said, sighing with exasperation. "What is one plus one?"

"Two!"

"That's right. Now, two plus two?"

"Four."

"Good. What is four plus four?"

I hesitated. "Eight."

"Yes. Now go back to your seat and study the next page of figures and we'll go over them."

I flounced back to my desk. I opened my book and gazed at the numbers on the pages. I hated arithmetic. I didn't understand the concepts of pluses and minuses and divides and multiplies. I could add as long as I could use ten fingers and ten toes. If more than that, I would put down rulers, pencils, erasers, whatever was available. I would then proceed to count them as additional appendages. Arithmetic was definitely not my strong point.

Miss Jenkins and daddy were deep in conversation. I could well imagine what she was telling him. I was happy to see daddy there, waiting to take me home but I was not happy to be kept after school and to have daddy find out.

I continued my contemplation of the hated numbers.

"Stella, come up and let's finish this lesson," Miss Jenkins said. "You can go home right after we finish this page."

I shuffled up the aisle to my place front and center of the blackboard. Daddy and Miss Jenkins sat a few rows behind me and waited.

I looked at the first set of numbers on the board. I silently mouthed the numbers.
I looked up at them and down; up; down. "Eight and eight is sixteen!" I looked up and down and up again.

"Sixteen and sixteen is thirty-two!" I looked up; I looked down.

"Stella, stop! Why are you looking down at your handkerchief?"

She walked over to me and held out her hand. "Give me the handkerchief, please."

"No, no, I blew my nose on it; it's dirty," I advised her.

"Now; the handkerchief now."

I was cornered. I was trapped. I was doomed. But I still held on to my little handkerchief.

I felt daddy's strong hand on my shoulder, turning me around to face him. "Stella, give me that," he commanded.

I complied. I placed the handkerchief in his outstretched hand. He smoothed it out placed it on top of Miss Jenkins' desk. Daddy and Miss Jenkins bent over and examined my handkerchief. There, amid the embroidered flowers were penciled:

8+8=16 16+16=32 32+32=64 64x2=128 128-28+10=110 ....

I heard daddy roar. “Stella; you cheated! My daughter, a cheat!”

He continued ranting and raving as Miss Jenkins tried to restore calm. “Now, now; let’s not get too upset,” she said. “Stella is having problems with arithmetic. I kept her after school. She’s never cheated before and I don’t think she will again. Will you, Stella?” she asked, glaring at me with her steel-blue eyes. Daddy continued blustering and I commenced to cry.

Miss Jenkins picked up my handkerchief and handed it to me. “Here; wipe your tears and blow your nose. That is what handkerchiefs are for. Not for cheating, not ever, ever, do you understand?”

“Y-y-yes.ssss” I stuttered, tears running down my face. “I promise to study; I promise to ask daddy to help me. I don’t want to be a bad girl.”

Daddy came over to me and put my hand into his. “Thank you, Miss Jenkins; thank you. Stella will never cheat again.” We walked out the school room door, down the creaky wooden hallway to the front door. I couldn’t wait to get out and breathe the fresh air and see the sky again.

“Now,” daddy said, “every day after school we’ll study your numbers together. Every day, understood?”

“Yes, daddy, yes,” I promised, relishing the time we would be spending together but hating the reason. Would I ever learn? Would I ever remember what plus and minus and subtract and divide meant? Was I meant to be a failure?

I started skipping beside daddy as we walked back home. I would show daddy how smart I was. I would let him help me until I no longer needed his help. No shame in admitting defeat. That was better than being a cheat.

I had learned a valued lesson.

Despite my assertiveness, I was basically a shy child. I especially disliked dressing up in costumes, having my picture taken or calling attention to myself in any manner, much to my mother's consternation.

A COWBOY'S TALE OF WOE

I was hiding under the chair, the burgundy velour one, daddy's favorite chair by the window. It was a big chair, with lots of room beneath it for me to hide. I felt safe there.

Shouts of joy sounded from outside and I wanted to run to the window to see all of my friends and be part of the excitement; yet, I was afraid of that excitement. A photographer was visiting the neighborhood, taking pictures of children draped in cowboy attire, perched on top of a pony.....a live pony!

Momma was looking for me and I curled up in a little ball, rolling back to the furthermost corner under the chair. I heard momma's footsteps coming closer and closer. I peeped from under the chair and I sensed her wrath before I even saw her. I rolled further back, disappearing into the darkness.

Suddenly, a hand grabbed my arm, pulling me back into the reality of the moment. Momma ordered me to stand up. Sensing her exasperation, I obeyed. I bent my head in feigned remorse, avoiding eye contact, waiting to see how the scenario would play out.

I was led outside to stand on the steps and wait my turn. I didn't want to put on that silly, ugly cowboy outfit. I didn't want to be a cowboy. Momma combed my hair, wiped the tears from my face and straightened my sweater. I heard the clip-clopping of the pony's hooves as he was led up the street by the photographer. They were coming straight at me. I turned, heading for the front door and a mad dash to safety when momma grabbed me by the back of my sweater. Pulling me towards her, she grasped my hand, forcing me to stand beside her. "Why don't you want to have your picture taken?", she asked. "Just think, you can be a cowboy. We can send pictures to your grandmother." I was not impressed. I would not wear that silly outfit.

The photographer stopped in front of our house and smiled at me. I scowled back at him. He came towards me with leather chaps, a red bandanna scarf and a big cowboy hat. “Hmmmm,” I thought; “I might make a good cowboy.” But I wouldn’t give in that easily. I buried my head in momma’s dress, sniffling and sobbing. “No cowboy; no cowboy,” I wailed.

The chaps were quickly thrown on and tied around my waist. The bandanna was secured around my neck and the hat was plopped firmly on my head. Before I had time to resist, I felt myself being lifted and quickly placed firmly on the saddle. The pony took a few sidesteps and I clasped the harness with both hands. The photographer settled the pony down, patted me on the shoulder and told me to sit still and smile my very best smile.

Okay, you asked for it, I thought. I lifted the hat, waving it in the air, smiling wide, flashing wide blank spaces where two front teeth were missing, and yelled, “Hi-ho, Silver!”

Weeks later, the pictures arrived. Momma quickly tore the envelope open and there I was, the best cowboy on Franklin Street. What action, what style, what bravery!

“Ride’em, cowgirl!”

Life was good, but my parents' marriage still was not without its problems. My father continued to work long hours and sought to spend his leisure time in the coffee shops and the backroom of the shoe-repair shop where the bachelors hosted nightly poker games. Poker became an obsession. The marriage became strained with my father's absences, his gambling and my mother's complaints. I was often the "go-between." I remember it well.

THE REFEREE

I remember.

I'm seven years old and standing in the middle of the bedroom. The harsh beams of the overhead light penetrate my sleep-swollen eyes. Daddy is standing in front of the dresser, the one with the three mirrors I like to stand in front of to see a triplicate of myself. He ties and reties his necktie until he gets it just right. He tucks in his shirt and tightens his belt. I stare at him. Momma is curled into a tiny ball on the far side of the bed and she's crying. I stare at her and she motions for me to come to her. I slide across the shiny floor and sit on the edge of the bed, averting my eyes from her tear-streaked face. I look down at my bare toes, my bunny slippers lost somewhere under my bed. I count my toes….one….two….three……anything to avoid the scenario unfolding before me.

Momma reaches out to hug me. In a whisper, she asks me to go and ask daddy to stay home. I jump off the bed and slide back across the floor. I stand by daddy. He is a big man and I am in awe of him. I tap him on the leg and he looks down at me as he brushes his hair. "Don't go," I whimper. "Don't go; please stay? Momma is sad."

His eyes are averted from the mirror and he focuses on me. His eyes are mesmerizing, deep brown, almond-shaped and hypnotic. "Do you love me?" I ask. He smiles at me and I feel warm all over. I squiggle my toes; he loves me! "Do you love momma? She loves you. Stay?"

He turns abruptly and walks out into the hallway and down the stairs. The front door slams. Daddy is gone. Momma sobs and I lean against the bed and I pat her cheek.

"Don't cry, momma; don't cry."

WITH THIS RING.....

The small square black velvet box had been placed on the dining room table. For two days, I stared at it, touched it, stroked the soft velvet covering and wondered what it held. Although curiosity was always a strong force within me, I knew this was not for me to open.

For two days, momma walked in and out of the dining room, going about her daily routine and not once did she stop to pick up the box. Every evening, daddy came home and on his way to the kitchen would glance at the box, ribbon still intact, still unopened. I puzzled over their actions and wondered how could momma not be the least bit curious?

Dinner was again a silent affair. Momma served daddy and me before bringing her plate to the table to join us. I glanced from one to the other, failing to make eye contact. Momma pushed the food around on her plate, taking only an occasional bite. Daddy ate hurriedly and abandoned us for his newspaper and cigarette in the living room. Not one word had been exchanged; not one glance. I finished dinner and silently gazed at momma, not knowing what to say. I wanted to go outside to play with my friends but felt that momma needed me there with her although I did not understand why. She sighed. She stacked the dishes and walked towards the sink. I followed.

"Momma," I said, "what's wrong?". She continued staring out of the window over the sink and I noticed a tear shining on her cheek. I patted her hand. She said nothing.

I tiptoed towards the living room and stood in the doorway. Daddy was engrossed with the latest news in the paper and did not glance my way. I went closer and stood behind his chair. I hugged him and whispered, "Daddy, what's wrong?" He put his arm out, pulling me to the front of his chair and stroked my arm.

"Don't worry," he said.

I persisted. "What's wrong? Why is momma crying?" Daddy averted his eyes from my questioning ones and retreated behind the paper.

I stood there, flashes of memory filtering through my head. I remembered daddy coming home the other night. It was very late and I had been in bed for hours. The slam of the door had awakened me and I had pulled the covers over my head, breathing quietly, waiting for whatever was to come. I remembered his footsteps on the stairs and down the hallway to their bedroom. I remembered the increased volume of their voices, escalating into muffled sobs from momma and gruff undertones from daddy. I had squirmed further down under the covers, silently praying to my personal God to make them stop. I was afraid. Their voices continued into the night, louder, softer; then, silence punctuated with momma's occasional sobs. I remembered throwing off the covers and padding my way down the hall and into the bedroom.

"Stop! Stop!," I shrieked. I remember shivering, both from cold and from fright. My nightgown had twisted around my ankles, my hair was standing up in tufts and my face was wet with tears and pale from fear. "Stop, please stop," I whispered as I crawled onto their bed. Momma then walked over to me to pull me into the circle of her arms. Daddy stood there, tall and silent, staring, not knowing what to do.

"I love you, momma; I love you, daddy. Please don't fight."

Momma had glanced at daddy, her look conveying messages words could not relay. Daddy then walked over to the bed and leaned over to kiss me.

"Kiss momma, too," I demanded, giving him my sternest look. He gave her a perfunctory peck on the cheek and patted her arm. He lifted me from the bed and deposited me back in my room. He kissed my tear-stained face and told me everything would be all right.

"Promise?", I asked; "Promise," he replied.

The very next day, the black velvet box had appeared, but momma wouldn't open it. I had waited for two days and finally decided to take matters into my own hands. I had to make things right. This had gone on long enough; tonight was the night for action. I snatched the box from the table and ran into the kitchen.

"Here," I said, forcing the box into momma's hands. "Open it!" I crossed my arms and stood boldly before her, daring her to disobey my command. "Open!"

She slowly untied the silver ribbon, placing it aside on the table for future use. She stroked the luxurious black velvet and slowly released the catch on the box. The lid flipped open and there amid the white satin rested the most beautiful ring I had ever seen. There was a diamond in the center with rubies on either side.

"Ohhhhh! Pretty!," I exclaimed. "Put it on, momma; put it on!" I hopped around her, grinning, making faces, anything to produce a smile on her forlorn face. She took the ring from the box and placed it on her finger. It captured the light from overhead, sending sprays of glorious color out into the room. My eyes widened in wonder. It was a magic ring! Momma put the ring back into the box and clutching it in her fist walked into the living room, directly towards daddy.
She tapped him on the arm and put out her hand, the box resting on her palm. Daddy looked at her in puzzlement.

"Open the box," she said. He did. "Put it on my finger," she demanded. He did. She kissed him shyly. He kissed her back. I beamed; I skipped; I was so happy. Momma and daddy were in love again!

****

The ring is mine now. It still sparkles and shines and I cherish this ring more than any other I have. Momma gave it to me years ago, along with her love and wishes for happiness. She assured me it was still a magic ring; I believe it.

My mother's creative talents provided me with the latest in fashion. A blue cape was a special possession of mine.

THE MAGIC CAPE

"There, it's finished!", momma said, shaking stray pieces of thread from her lap. The droning of the sewing machine came to a slow stop, the needle puncturing final stitches into the blue material.

Light filtered in through the curtained window, showering rainbow dots of color on the ceiling and walls, decorating an otherwise dull room. This was momma's sewing room, a room for designing, cutting, stitching, ironing; a room for creating, nothing more. I would often perch on the edge of the wide window sill and watch momma push yards of material through the machine, the needle pulsating up, down, up, down, as her hands guided the fabric, her feet pushing the treadle faster and faster. .

"Stand up," momma said. I quickly jumped from the sill and stood up straight, tummy tucked in, shoulders back, heels together. She draped the blue cape around my shoulders. Soft folds encircled my skinny little body, cascading down to my bony and bandaged knees, enveloping me in deep blue splendor. I buttoned the top button, a glittering gold button, and adjusted the collar. I inspected the bright red lining, the pocket slits where I could poke my arms through when it wasn't too cold and the huge hem that insured future years of wear. Momma had done a wonderful job creating my cape.

Easter was early this year and momma had been in a hurry to finish the many sewing projects. Every year, momma would sew a special Easter outfit for me. This year, the cape was to be the latest addition to my wardrobe. I had begged for a cape all of my own after seeing Shirley Temple wearing one in her latest movie. I had loved the way the cape furled and twirled and I wanted to be another Shirley Temple. Momma promised, momma created, momma delivered.

Standing before my favorite three-way mirror, I admired the many images reflected back at me. I twirled, I swirled and the cape furled out around me. I flung one half of the cape over my left shoulder, the red satin lining now visible, a vibrant garnet slash across the dark blue wool. In my imagination, I was now a Red Cross nurse, crossing the battlefield, bringing hope, trust and salvation to the wounded. Or, I could be an airline hostess, calming fears of weary travelers. I could be a movie star, grandly strutting to front stage and the waiting Oscar, or a famous opera star taking a bow before an adoring audience. I could be anything I wanted to be. This was my magic cape.

Magic cape! There was my answer! I would wear my cape this very day. The magic cape would give me style, flair and even the fearlessness I needed for that afternoon. My cousins, Nick and George, visiting from Savannah, Georgia, had reluctantly agreed to take me with them to the Saturday matinee, a western. I had never seen a western movie before and had only heard about cowboys and Indians, fighting and shooting. Admitting my ignorance was not easy for I wanted to be accepted. I wanted to go, but I was afraid. Cowboys and Indians sounded very scary. But now, the blue cape would envelop me, surround me, comfort me with the courage I needed.

It was time to go. Clutching our movie allowances, we headed for the neighborhood movie house. With Nick on one side and George on the other, I strutted. The cape swirled around me, garnet lining flashing in the wind. I was invincible; I was Dale Evans, with Roy Rogers on one side and Gene Autry on the other.

In my caped splendor!
left to right- my mother's cousins, Angliki and Maria, Momma, me (front), Daddy

The pull of two cultures often caused me great pain. I never voiced my discontent aloud but even at an early age, I could tell I was "different" and the refrain of "nice Greek girls don't do that" echoed in my mind constantly.

VALENTINES I NEVER RECEIVED

Valentine's Day. I couldn't wait to get to school and place valentines in the box. We had helped Miss Martin, our third-grade teacher, make the box days ago. White paper covered the box. Red hearts were drawn on all sides of the box. A slot was cut by Miss Martin in the top of the box, ready to receive all the valentines we had made to send to our friends. I had my stack of cards ready, tightly bound by a rubber band and placed on top of my book bag. Momma helped me into a gray corduroy dress she had made for me to wear on this day. Little red felt hearts circled the neckline and I felt so special.

Gathering the valentines and book bag, I quickly walked to school, eager to deposit the cards and wait impatiently for them to be delivered. I crossed my fingers as I walked, silently praying I would get some valentines. .

I entered Room 112 and there in the middle of the room was The Box. It shimmered under the glow of the overhead light. The scattered scarlet hearts decorating all four sides seemed to pulsate, sending out messages of "I love you." I pushed my cards through the slot, making sure they fell safely to the bottom of the box and walked to my desk to wait.

Time seemed endless. The box seemed to dominate every inch of the room and absorbed all of our attention and energies. Miss Martin did her best to proceed with the day's lesson plan and to contain the attention span of 20 eager children. Finally, recess time arrived. Now the box would be opened; now we would get our valentines! I wiggled and squirmed, wondering what I would do if no valentines were meant for me. Slowly, Miss Martin lifted the box top, turned the box over, thumping the contents out onto the table. My eyes grew wider as I saw an avalanche of valentines tumbling out. Surely, some were for me?

Finally the box was empty; all the valentines had been delivered.

Twenty pairs of hands ripped into envelopes, scattering paper everywhere, huge snowflakes of paper descending onto the bare wooden floor. Squeals of joy, of embarrassment and of surprise filled the room. Shy looks were exchanged; toothless grins shared. A warmth filled me from within; I had valentines! I was so happy! I couldn't wait to show momma and daddy.

Walking home, hugging the satisfaction inside me, I suddenly remembered what daddy had said. "No valentines! I don't want to see you with valentines from boys! No boys; no valentines!" The bubble of rapture burst, and the echo of "No valentines; no boys," repeated itself with every step that brought me closer to home.

I slowly tore my valentines into small, ragged pieces, throwing them to the wind, watching the pieces flutter to the ground to be trampled on and forgotten. I held the very last valentine and looked at it longingly. It, too, had to disappear. I shredded it and threw it to the ground. One piece remained in my hands, the one with the words, "I luv U - Stanley." I slipped the piece under the cuff of my sweater, scrunching it down into the folds of the sleeve and silently walked into my house.

Daddy was sitting in the living room in his usual spot by the window, waiting for me. I slammed the door shut and slid out of my coat, careful not to pull on my sweater sleeve. "No, daddy, I got no valentines," I said, before he had time to ask. "No valentines," I repeated. He looked at me and smiled, and turned back to his newspaper.

I walked slowly towards my room, caressing the small piece of paper hidden within the folds of my sweater. The words "I luv U" burned their way into my heart and soul; I was loved!

I was an only child and friends and neighborhood dogs and cats filled the void. I was compassionate and cared a great deal for those not able to care for themselves.

A CAT TALE

School was out for the day and another school week had ended. I felt free with a whole weekend before me. If I did my homework as soon as I got home, I pondered, I wouldn't have to worry about it for two whole days. Yep, that's what I would do. I shifted books in my arms to a more comfortable position and turned the corner, headed for home.

I heard footsteps behind me and stopped to look around. There was Joanne, running, huffing and puffing, to catch up with me. "Hi," she whooped, "wait up!"

I waited for her to catch her breath and we soon resumed walking together in perfect stride, not missing a step. We discussed homework. We exchanged answers to expected test questions. We laughed at each other's jokes. We were such good friends.

"Wait, Stella, let's stop here a minute," Joanne said. She plopped down on the sidewalk and sat on the curb, legs straight out, leaning back on her arms. "I don't want to go home yet," she said. "Here, have some candy," she offered, tempting me with a chocolate bar.

I took the candy and slowly peeled off the wrapper. I gently moved the foil to unearth the glorious chocolate beneath. The aroma filled my nostrils and I couldn't wait for the chocolate to melt in my mouth. "Ummmm," I uttered, as the chocolate worked its magic. "Ummmm," I repeated.

Joanne and I sat in happy silence. It was a quiet street with few people or cars to interrupt the stillness. It was late spring. New leaves were sprouting on the trees and flowers were making their appearance. The air smelled fresh and clean. And only one more month of school. Hallelujah!

"What'cha thinkin', Stella?" asked Joanne.

"Nothin'," I replied, still savoring the last morsels of chocolate.

Silence.

"Look, look," screamed Joanne suddenly, pointing wildly to the opposite side of the street.

"What? Where?" I asked.

"There," she said, continuing to point in the general area of the wide street across from us.

I soon heard a mewling sound and saw the lower branches of a bush move. From the dark interior of the bush came a cat and two tiny kittens. "See?" asked Joanne in a hushed voice, "See?"

I nodded and watched in awe as the momma cat nudged the kittens. She meowed as if to say, "follow me." The kittens scrambled and tumbled behind their mother as she strutted before them, tail held high, a beacon for them to follow.

"There are two kittens," Joanne observed.

"I know; I can count!" I snipped back. I was too busy watching the three-cat parade for nonsense talk.

"Two," she continued. "One for you and one for me."

I turned to her, eyes wide in wonder. "Do you think?" I asked in wonder. "Maybe they belong to somebody."

"Nah," Joanne replied. "They're not wearing any collars."

The kittens stopped at the curb, gauging the distance down to the street. Momma cat had already stepped off and turned to hiss at them to hurry. Heads down, they looked at the dark sea of asphalt before them. Heads up, they looked at each other. Together, they gazed at their momma. She glared at them and meowed further instructions. She squatted at the curb and waited for her kittens to gather their courage.

"I want the black one," Joanne advised me; "you can have the gray one."

"Okay," I said. "But how do we get them?"

Joanne knelt down on the pavement. "Psssst, psssst; here, kitty, here, kitty," Joanne said in a soft, coaxing voice.

"Pssst, pssst," I echoed as I squatted down on the concrete pavement.

One momma cat and two kittens stared at us.

We continued calling and slowly the momma cat slinked her way towards us. The kittens tumbled onto the asphalt. Dazed, they shook their fuzzy heads and stood on wobbly legs. They began to follow their mother's footsteps.

"Okay, the black one's yours, and I'll catch the gray one," I instructed. "But what happens to the mother cat?"

"I don't know, but she can take care of herself; the kittens are babies and need someone to look after them real good," replied Joanne.

I processed the information and reluctantly came to the same conclusion.

"Pssst, psssst," I uttered. "Pssst, psssst; here kitty, kitty, here kitty; come here," I whispered. The gray fuzz ball of a kitten stopped in its tracks and looked at me. It turned direction and started to cross the street in a haphazard diagonal line, its little legs wobbling as it tried to run towards me. I bent over to brush dirt and leaves from my skirt in preparation of welcoming my kitten into my lap and waiting arms.

"Whoosh," I heard. "Sscreeeeee-ch," I heard. "Thump," I heard.

I stood up and closed my eyes. I didn't want to see what I knew was there. I heard the muffled sound of a car speeding down the street, off into the unknown distance. I heard a hurtful sound of a kitten meow. I heard the crying of a mother over her baby. It was death happening, but in a feline world. I ran into the street as Joanne followed me. I knelt down by the injured kitten. It was the gray one, my kitten. The mother cat circled, nudging the other kitten to safety by the curbside. The gray kitten was but a little ball of fuzz. Its cloudy blue eyes looked at me and pleaded for no more pain. I touched its tiny head and stroked its fuzzy back. It purred and then closed its eyes. Silence. It was no more.

I picked up the kitten and cradled it in my arms. I sat on the curb and wailed in mourning and anger and disbelief.

Joanne sat beside me, her arm encircling my shoulder as she murmured words of comfort. I continued to rock back and forth, back and forth, cradling and hugging a dead kitten. A kitten that hadn't had a chance to be mine. A kitten that would have been pampered and loved and cared for in such a loving way. But it was not to be. And I cried for it as I had never cried before.

****

It was years before I was ready for a kitten of my own. Ironically, it was a gray kitten and I named her "Sassy."

Cultural differences became even more apparent as I grew older. Sunday outings with momma and daddy became ordeals and my efforts to escape were to no avail. Good Greek girls did as their parents said.

GRAPE LEAVES OF WRATH

It was a warm Sunday afternoon and time for the weekly Sunday drive into the country. Momma looked forward to these excursions, the highlight of her week, away from the drudgery of cooking, cleaning and watching over me. Daddy needed some time away from his restaurant, a chance to get away from the many responsibilities and problems. So, the Sunday drives had been initiated. I was not too happy with the outings, but who had asked me?

Daddy sat in the car, honking the horn impatiently, sending messages to momma to hurry up. Momma scurried around the house, checking to see that all lights were turned off, the toaster disconnected and the iron and ironing board put away. I sat forlornly on the living room sofa, dressed in a freshly ironed pinafore and waited for the dreaded Sunday drive to begin.

"Come on, come on, Stella," momma said. "Daddy's getting tired of waiting for us. Let's go." She urged me down from the sofa and guided me out the front door. She closed it and double-checked to see that it was locked. She glanced at the living room windows to ensure they were tightly closed. Satisfied that the homestead was secured, she pushed me ahead, down the front porch steps to the waiting Oldsmobile.

Momma placed me in the back seat of the car and locked the doors. She settled into the front seat and sighed a sigh of relief. A few hours in the pastoral countryside promised her the escape she needed. Daddy started the car and slowly pulled away from the curb and headed out of town towards the quiet rural splendors of Washington County, Maryland.

Silence prevailed as momma leaned her head back onto the headrest. She shut her eyes and savored the tranquillity of the afternoon. Daddy stared ahead, intent on driving, as the car sped up and down the hilly country roads.

I moped and sighed and wished I were anywhere but there. I was bored. I wanted to be with my friends or even my little kitten, Sassy. Anything but this, anything. I did not enjoy the Sunday drives because of their ultimate purpose.

"Stop, Chris, stop. Look over there," momma said, pointing to a large empty field on her right.

Daddy brought the car to a slow stop and agreed with momma that the field did indeed look promising.

Momma jumped out of the car and walked briskly to the edge of the field. Gnarled grapevines covered the fence, spilling over from one side and down the other. Purple grapes peeked from beneath huge leaves and a sweet pungent aroma filled the air. "Okay," she said, "let's see what we can gather here."

She handed me a little basket and showed me where I should begin. She and daddy walked to the opposite end of the fence and began picking the tender leaves from the vine. Occasionally, they consumed over-ripened fruit, sweet juices trickling down their chins. They were having a wonderful time.

I shuffled along the path, careful not to step in grapes that had fallen from their perch. I began to pick the small, tender leaves just as momma had taught me.

The warm sun on my back soon soothed me. The chirping of birds cheered me and the solitude lulled me into a feeling of contentment. I continued pulling leaves off of the vines, filling the little basket and pocketed a cluster of purple grapes for the ride home. I began humming, lost in my thoughts. I pushed away the fear of being seen by any of my friends and began to enjoy the peaceful afternoon.

Honk! Honk! Honk! The sound startled me and I turned to find the source of the disruption. A car approached at a leisurely pace as I stood by the fence, basket in hand, knees dirty from kneeling on the grass, hair wilted and face gleaming with the sweat of hard work.

“Hey, Stella; whatcha’ doin’?”

I caught a glimpse of my secret crush. He was grinning and waving at me from the rear window. All I could do was stare as the car sped down the road, slowly disappearing over the next hilly slope.

I was beyond embarrassment. I was mortified. There I was, a peasant picking grape leaves with my mother and father. Grape leaves! Who ever heard of picking grape leaves? And with both parents, as if I had no friends and nothing better to do. How would I face him the next day in school? What would he think of me? Who would he tell?

Momma and daddy continued picking leaves, oblivious to my disturbed state. I threw the basket on the ground, the carefully picked grape leaves scattered helter-skelter over the matted grass. I ran to the car and jumped into the back seat. I crouched on the floor of the car, hiding from further sightings. My life was ruined.

I was hot, sweaty, hungry and tired. All I wanted to do was go home and wallow in my misery. Momma had a thermos of cold water with her but I would not leave the car. I suffered in silence.

Eventually, momma and daddy returned to the car and placed the many baskets of grape leaves in the trunk. Momma peered into the car and saw me lying on the backseat. “What’s wrong, Stella?” she asked in an anxious voice. “Are you tired or sick or what?”

“Nothing; just tired. I don’t know. Just leave me alone!” I moaned as I turned and burrowed into the soft velour of the back seat.

Momma took her place in the front seat of the car as daddy turned the key and brought the car to life.

“What a nice day,” commented momma.

“Yes,” agreed daddy. “And we have lots of grape leaves to store. Lots of “dolmades,” right, Stella?”

My life was ruined and all they could think of was “dolmades”! Who would understand my grief? Who would erase the stigma of the peasant from my soul?

“We’ll do this again next Sunday,”chirped momma, content with her Sunday outing.

“Yes, we can,” agreed daddy, “and maybe we can find some dandelion greens to pick, too.”

Momma smiled and began humming, already anticipating an outing seven days away.

I burrowed further into the shelter of the back seat of the car. The day was over as well as my life and no one would ever understand.

****

Ironically, “dolmades” are my favorite Greek food. The succulent grape leaves wrap morsels of meat blended with rice and spices into neat little bundles. The creamy béchamel sauce gently covers them. Indeed, food for the gods. I will, however, never forget my grape leaves gathering days.

I was pulled into auditioning for a school play by a loyal friend. I wanted her to have the part with all my heart and great was my disappointment when this was not to be.

THE STAR

Auditions for "Hansel and Gretel" had just been announced. The fourth grade class at Antietam Elementary School would perform in four weeks and all aspiring actors and actresses were encouraged to try out. The poster announced:

"AUDITIONS TODAY 1 P.M. AUDITORIUM

If interested, advise classroom teachers and obtain permission to miss afternoon classes.

Hansel -	Boy to portray a brave 9-year-old; dark hair; strong personality; lead role
Gretel -	Petite girl to portray a 7-year-old, preferably blonde; shy personality; second lead role
Witch -	Girl to portray the Wicked Witch; not a large speaking part; must be able to be "scary"
Hunter -	Boy to portray a hunter in the woods; non-speaking part
Crowd -	4 boys and 4 girls to be in crowd scene
Scenery/ Props -	Artistic talent needed to design sets and costumes
Sound -	Musical talent needed to suggest and provide background music and sounds"

Best friend Joanne and I pushed our way through the giggling girls crowded around the bulletin board to get a better look at the poster. "Look," Joanne said, "we're putting on a play - Hansel and Gretel! Let's try out, Stella."

I looked at her in amazement. Try out for a play? Me? I was too shy and quiet to appear before a critical audience of parents and peers. I shook my head and said, "No!"

"Come on, it'll be fun," Joanne countered. "I'm going; come with me. Come on, at least we'll get out of class."

Now that had merit to it. Hating history class as I did, I reluctantly agreed and promised to meet Joanne in the auditorium at 1 p.m.

Mrs. Martin stood at the open door to the auditorium. She checked permission slips from the aspiring actors and actresses who had gathered. She took a second glance as I handed her my permission slip. "Stella? I'm surprised to see you here," she said. I smiled shyly and made my way to the front of the auditorium and to the waiting Joanne.

Joanne wanted the part of Gretel but her chubby frame and dark hair wouldn't fit the part. Not wanting to be a bit player in the crowd scene, she decided to try out for the part of the Wicked Witch. She practiced making scary faces and screeching sounds, waving her arms in a threatening way. I was impressed and told her so. "You'd be a great witch," I said. "I know you'll get the part."

Finally, it was time for tryouts for the part of the witch. Joanne walked towards the front of the auditorium and up to center stage. She put on the costume, read the lines and acted out the part. She was great, just as I had predicted. Mrs. Martin smiled and thanked her and then peered anxiously out into the by now sparsely populated auditorium. "Do we have anyone else interested in trying out for the Wicked Witch?" she asked. Silence. Chairs squeaked as impatient students settled into more comfortable positions. "Anyone?" Mrs. Martin repeated. "We need to have more than one person trying out for all parts." Continued silence.

Joanne tapped Mrs. Martin on the shoulder and offered her a solution to the current dilemma.

"Stella? You think Stella wants to try out for this part?" asked an incredulous Mrs. Martin in a harsh whisper. "Stella?"

"Yes," nodded Joanne. "She told me she wanted to."

Poor Mrs. Martin. What to do. An entire student body and only one person interested in this very important character part. She had to have at least two auditions, but somehow Stella did not seem to have the flair necessary to carry the part.

It was nearing 3 o'clock and auditions had to be over by 3:45 p.m., the end of the school day. Mrs. Martin reluctantly decided to ask for the suggested audition, knowing full well there would be no competition for Joanne.

"Stella, please come up here," she directed. I sat up in my seat, startled into reality. It had been a long, boring afternoon and I had escaped into my daydreams. What could Mrs. Martin possibly want with me?

Never one to question authority, I made my way up the steps and stood by Mrs. Martin. "Stella, we want you to try out for the part of the Wicked Witch. Joanne told me how much you wanted the part." I froze. What? I turned around in search of my so-called friend but she was nowhere to be found.

Mrs. Martin handed me the script, explaining that the spoken parts for the witch were highlighted in red. I was to look over the lines and be prepared to read for the part. A sense of panic overtook me and cold sweat broke out all over me. I couldn't move, but I couldn't stay, either. What was I going to do?

"Quickly now, Stella," Mrs. Martin ordered, "we have to be out of here by 3:45 so let's start. Here, put this on," she said as she handed me the costume. A long, ragged black dress was pulled on and a rope belt wound around my waist. A cape was thrown over my shoulders and a pointed hat placed on my head. Fortunately, my protruding ears kept the hat from sliding down my face and I peered out from under the brim at the smirking faces in the audience staring back at me.

I clutched the script tightly to my chest as I stepped forward to front stage. Mrs. Martin suggested I picture the yet-to-be-scenery. "The gingerbread house will be here," she said, pointing to left stage. "Trees and bushes will be here as part of the forest and over there will be the path leading to the house from the forest." She looked at me to gauge my comprehension. "Can you see that in your mind?" she asked. I nodded.

Mrs. Martin said she would read the parts for the other characters and prompt me when it was time for me to speak or cackle. I stood frozen in place, realizing there was no way out and I had to do this.

I removed myself mentally from my present state and visualized a witch. How would she look? How would she walk? What would her voice sound like? How would she cackle, laugh, screech? A metamorphosis was taking place. I was becoming a witch.

Mrs. Martin pointed at me to begin my lines. I shuffled to the chalk mark on the stage, my back bent, my head lowered as a slow cackle emerged from my parched lips. "Hee, hee, hee," I shrieked in glee as I rubbed my hands together. "Soon they will be here, my little Hansel and Gretel," I announced in a high-pitched voice. I looked out at the audience and glowered at them, my eyes wild, my lips quivering and covered with saliva. "Hee, hee, hee, they will be mine soon."

Mrs. Martin gazed in awe. She had never seen such a transformation. My immersion in the part was so complete, she couldn't believe what she was witnessing. She prompted me through the rest of the act as I became more and more engrossed in my character.

Finally, it was over. Mrs. Martin announced there there would be no more auditions and selections would be announced the next day. She walked over to where I stood, perspiration glazing my face, hair matted and hanging from under the pointed hat. I took off the costume and handed it to Mrs. Martin. She smiled at me and said, "Good job,

Stella" and patted me on the back.

I ran off stage and out of the auditorium in search of cool air, a water fountain and my traitor friend, Joanne.

Cast selections were announced at class assembly the next day. Mrs. Martin began reading the names and I clapped loudly, happy that such good choices had been made. I punched Joanne on her arm and whispered, "Your name is next; I just know it!"

"And now, the part of the Wicked Witch," Mrs. Martin began. "This part, although not a large speaking part, is a major character in the play. A great deal relies on actions rather than words. I must say we truly have a wonderful witch among us. Stand up, Stella."

Joanne shrieked in joy. "I knew it, I knew it!" I sat in stunned silence. "Get up," Joanne ordered as she pulled me up from the seat. I stood on wobbly legs and knew not what to do. I had fleeting thoughts of stuffing Joanne in a locker, but too late now. I smiled nervously at Mrs. Martin and my cheering classmates. I said a silent prayer asking for intestinal fortitude to carry this off.

Four weeks of rehearsals were over and opening night was here. The hum of talk and laughter filtered through the heavy stage curtains as the auditorium began to fill. I paced nervously back and forth. This was not a rehearsal, this was the real thing and I was plenty scared.

Hansel and Gretel sat on a small bench backstage. They were laughing and talking and totally at ease. I made my way over to them and perched on the edge of the bench. "Are you scared?" I asked. "No," answered Gretel. "Nah," said Hansel. "Me neither," I lied.

I peeped through the slight opening of the stage curtain and reeled with the impact of a full house. Not one empty seat! I surveyed the audience trying to find my mother, hoping against hope that she would not be there. I took a last look at the crowd and finally spotted her sitting in the section reserved for family members of the cast. She had come after all, much to my dismay.

The lights dimmed and a hush came over the auditorium. The stage curtains creaked open, revealing a verdant forest surrounding a crooked gingerbread house. Background music swelled to a crescendo and Mrs. Martin began narrating the scene.

Hansel and Gretel played their parts splendidly, talking, crying and screaming when and where needed, as practiced. I, the Wicked Witch, was a cackling, grotesque figure, eager to devour Hansel and Gretel. My white, wrinkled face, with a huge wart on the chin was frightening. Eyes were wide and wild and my lips smacked in anticipation of the tasty morsels Hansel and Gretel would make. Words were spoken in eerie tones; screeches and howls sent shivers up and down our collective spines. I was truly a witch as I whirled and twirled in my black robe and cape.

The play ended happily, as intended. The cast bowed to numerous encores as the audience cheered and clapped. The cast clasped hands and stood in a row, basking in the warmth of audience approval. It was exhilarating.

I changed into my clothes, tossing the black costume in a far corner backstage. I wiped my face clean of the awful makeup and made my way into the auditorium. Classmates hovered and quickly engulfed me. “Stella, you were great!” one said. “I thought you were shy,” commented another. “How did you learn to be such a good actress?” “Boy, I’m glad I don’t have to run into you in a dark alley” giggled another. I felt enveloped in warmth and friendship and I murmured my thanks as I made my way through the group. I saw Joanne waiting for me at the edge of the crowd and I waited to see what she had to say. I still hadn’t quite forgiven her for what she had done. “Hi, Stella,” she said quietly. “You are one great witch!” I laughed and tapped her on the arm as I continued walking.

I found momma sitting in the back of the auditorium, patiently waiting for me. “Hi, momma,” I said as I stood before her. She looked up at me and smiled a tremulous smile, her eyes glistening with tears. My, I thought, my acting must have really moved her and I figuratively patted myself on the back.

"How did you like the play?" I asked.

She started crying again. "You reminded me of my mother in that black dress," she said as she continued sobbing.

Yes, I could see the resemblance. I remembered my grandmother in her black, long dress, bent back, shuffling gait - yes, that was my grandmother. But where were my accolades? I was a star, couldn't momma see that?

I walked silently out of the auditorium into the night and waited for momma to join me.

My mother immersed herself in learning the customs of America and efforts were continuously made in every way to have me participate in all of the new traditions…or as many as "nice Greek girls" were allowed.

HURRAY FOR HALLOWEEN!!

"Ahh, look how pretty this turned out to be!" exclaimed momma as she pushed her chair back from the sewing machine. She held out the dress and admired it, shaking it loose from any stray threads.

She called out to me, eager for me to try on her latest creation. I reluctantly walked into the sewing room for the final fitting. I sat on the old blue velvet armchair that had been relegated to the sewing room and waited for further instructions.

The school Halloween party was to take place the following day and momma had labored over my costume for days. I had shown no interest in the project. Dressing up in silly costumes seemed totally absurd to me.

"Look, Stella, look at your costume," momma said. "Try it on so I can see if anything needs to be done before tomorrow. Stand up and try it on; come on, stand up," she urged.

I pulled off my sweater and struggled out of my corduroy pants, flinging them onto the armchair. Momma carefully slipped the dress over my head and guided its full gathered skirt to settle at my waistline. It was made of red cotton. It had full gathered sleeves and a round neckline. To my dismay, it fit. Momma stepped back to admire her creation. "Nice, very nice," she murmured.

Next, a white apron with appliquéd red tulips all around the hem was tied on over the red dress. Momma sighed her approval once more. I stood, sullen and quite unhappy.

"Now," said momma, "this will complete the outfit." She placed a white Dutch girl cap on my head, pulling it down tightly on my crown. The side flaps of the cap stuck out in starched splendor, anchored no less by my protruding ears. Tiny red tulips had been embroidered on each side of the cap and I was resplendent in my hand-crafted outfit. Momma was so happy with her handiwork and she gazed lovingly at me in my Halloween costume. I stood there, eyes downcast, totally mortified. I would have to walk to school the next day as the Dutch Girl. How embarrassing!

Next day became today and there was no avoiding the inevitable. The costume had been carefully ironed and starched by momma. It hung in my closet, waiting for me. I struggled into the dress and apron, tying the apron strings as best I could. Momma pinned the hat on me, securing it with four bobbypins to withstand any breeze that might tamper with it. I was ready for the party whether I wanted to go or not. I knew momma was happy with the costume she had made for me and she anticipated the good time she knew I would have. I didn't want to disappoint her, but I hated the costume, I hated the idea of walking to school as a Dutch Girl and I hated the idea of a party where everyone would be staring at me.

I snuggled into my navy wool coat and buttoned it all the way up to my chin in a vain effort to hide the costume. I stepped outside and began the short walk to school, a sorry sight to behold. There I was in a knee-length navy blue coat, with four inches of red dress flapping against my legs and a Dutch Girl cap waving in the breeze. I whimpered muffled sobs all the way to school and dreaded the encounter with friends and other students.

"Oh, Stella," I heard someone call. I turned a deaf ear and kept walking. "Stella, wait up." The voice sounded familiar and I slowed down. Joanne bounded up and stepped in stride with my silent walk.

"You look so good," she said. "That is really a great outfit."

"Oh, yeah? You think so?" I asked, turning a tear-stained face towards her.

"Are you crying?" she asked.

"No; got something in my eye," I replied. "You really like this costume?" I asked, needing verification.

"Yeah, I do. It's nice; so different. Where'd you get it?" she continued.

I held my head up high, cap wings waving in the breeze and smugly said, "My momma made it."

I had never been happier.

Being an only child, I "adopted" little Christy as my brother. Our mothers were best friends; we were both only children and so we became sister and brother. It was such fun to have a brother - someone I could fight with, just like all the other kids with siblings. How sad I was when Christy and his family eventually moved away.

WHEELS OF ADVENTURE

The little red tricycle was slowly wheeled into our backyard. A fire-engine red three-wheeler, with evidence of much wear and tear. Rust showed through where the paint had flaked off, the wheels were wobbly and the silver bell was rusted and silent. Not a pretty tricycle, but functional, and it was mine once again.

The bike had been on loan to Christy for several months without my consent. I had watched momma push the tricycle up the street to its new owner. Christy had quickly claimed possession and just as quickly I hated him.

Christy and his parents had recently moved to Hagerstown and lived three blocks away from us. Christy's momma and my momma were the best of friends and happy to be reunited again in the same town and same neighborhood. Christy and I, on the other hand, were meeting for the first time and our friendship was yet to be tested. Momma had offered to lend my tricycle to Christy, out of hospitality, generosity and friendship. Also, too many banged and bruised knees and torn dresses had convinced momma that the tricycle was a better toy for boys. The bike was for Christy to use.

Christy had been thrilled to have the bike. He was fiercely determined to get all the mileage he could out of it before it was returned. I had been content circling around and around in our back yard, or perhaps a quick trip to the corner candy store but no further. Christy, on the other hand, had places to visit and worlds to conquer. I watched him daily as he passed our house, plump little legs pumping the pedals furiously, wheels turning wildly as he made his way uptown. Uptown! I didn't even know uptown existed! Off he would go, pedaling up the hill, down the hill, across the street and finally careening wildly right into his daddy's store for a visit and a quest for candy or an extra nickel or two.

Christy's escapades were not to be tolerated. He was reprimanded, threatened and punished, to no avail. The flame of adventure burned too brightly for him to surrender. I watched his trips in awe, silently wishing that I, too, could be a part of them.

The day had finally come when Christy was forbidden further use of the little red tricycle. It had to be returned to its rightful owner. It was wheeled back into our backyard for my sole use and possession. I was cautioned not to let Christy see the bike. It had to be hidden behind the overgrown lilac bushes at the end of our yard. The little red bicycle had returned home.

I was soon circling the perimeter of our yard, content with my limited world. I relished the fact that Christy had been punished and was now without transportation.

Days later, the red tricycle was not to be found. I searched the bushes, the yard, the porch and found no trace of the tricycle. I ran to the garden gate and peered over the wooden slats. Whizzing by me was Christy on the red tricycle on his way uptown, the search for adventure still burning brightly within him, punishment be damned! He had stolen my bike. He was without remorse. He was free to roam the world again!

****

I don't recall what happened after that. Probably, the tricycle was given away to curtail Christy's wanderings and to prevent any meanderings on my part.

To this day, however, I still have a vision of Christy in his white sailor suit….white short pants, shirt with a navy collar and tie….furiously pedaling his way to the world beyond. Christy is now Chris, a husband, a father and a grandfather. The sense of wanderlust has been tamed somewhat. He is quietly enjoying retirement and the joys of rose gardening. But the spark of Christy is still there, the hint of mischief and the lure of adventure not totally extinguished.

Toys were few and summer camps were unknown. Our imaginations went wild and games were constantly invented and created to fill our summer days.

JUNGLE JANE

The heat blasted up from the sidewalk, gluing my soles to the brick sidewalk and almost melting the patent leather tops of my new sandals. Crinkled heat waves distorted my view and I squinted my eyes to better see. No one was in sight.

I twirled, spinning around and around on the toes of my new sandals, my skirt dipping and whirling in the breeze I generated. I came to an abrupt halt as I heard momma calling. "Stella…a…a…a…a.," followed by the dreaded clang of the little handbell she kept for such warnings. Momma knew I'd come running helter-skelter, if only to silence the embarrassing clamor of the bell.

Momma stood on the porch, bell in hand, ready for another ringing. I dashed up the steps, tripping on the last one, skinning an already scarred right knee. I looked up at her, peeking through tangled, uncombed bangs. A warning was about to be issued; I could tell.

"Stay on the porch; don't get dirty; comb your hair; pull up your socks"…. the familiar daily instructions. I nodded but heeded none of the requests. It was Sunday and company was coming soon. I had to make my debut. I had my favorite dress on, a peach-colored taffeta with a big sash ending in a floppy bow, its long streamers bouncing off my bottom when I walked. I loved that dress, but waiting for company on a Sunday afternoon was not what I wanted to do.

I walked to the edge of the sidewalk, stepped out into the street and dashed diagonally across to the nearby field. I knew just where to find my friends. I stomped through the high field grass, carefully lifting my skirt, remembering momma's admonishments to stay clean. I followed the little stream and came to the large oak tree at the edge of the bank. There, knee-high in muddy water were the cronies I had been searching for. A game of Tarzan and Jungle Jane was just beginning. They were almost finished choosing sides and I crossed my fingers and wished very, very hard. Let it be my turn to be Jungle

Jane, please, please, please, I begged.

Noel looked at me and I gave him my best smile. He was my next door neighbor and knew how very much I wanted to be the next, and best, Jungle Jane. Noel waved to me, yelling out my name as Jungle Jane to his Tarzan. I was in heaven! I zigzagged through the muddy path, oblivious to patent leather sandals and white socks. Claiming my title was all that mattered now. I grabbed the garbled rope, untwisting its length from around the lower branch of the oak tree. I gave it a good push to check its grip on the top-most branches. I clutched both fists around the rope, gave a big push and shrieked my best jungle yell. I swung out over the muddy water below, sailing to Tarzan waiting for me on the opposite shore.

Something went terribly wrong. I became airborne as my hands slithered down the length of the rope. I tried to grasp it again in its trajectory but it flew by me on its solo flight. I plummeted downward into the middle of the stream, at its muddiest deep. My peach taffeta skirt billowed out around me as I desperately tried to find sturdy ground for my sandaled feet. Rocks and twigs formed a shaky surface under me as I slithered my way towards the opposite bank. The water was clearer and cleaner by the shoreline and I scrunched down, soaking my taffeta dress free of the muddy remains of my journey. I wrung it out with both hands, squeezing as much water out of the folds of material as I could. I spun around and around, hoping the dizzying velocity would be a natural dryer for the dress. My friends stood around me, eyes wide open and mouths agape, secretly pleased it was me and not they in this Sunday afternoon calamity.

I shrugged my shoulders at them and started my journey home. They waved at me; Noel winked at me. One by one they shouted, “Bye, Jungle Jane; bye!”

That had to be the best Sunday I had ever had, despite the waiting punishment.

Being an only child did not provide me with whatever I wanted, despite the popular perception that only children were spoiled. I tried to get my way, but when told otherwise, I accepted without a fight. Sulk, I might, but talk back, never.

SWEATER GIRL

December, 1944. Shops glittered in anticipation of the holidays. Multi-colored lights blinked and twinkled between massive boughs of greenery. The Christmas tree stood in the center of the town square, towering over folks scurrying here and there. The tempo of the town had accelerated and the air was filled with an electric anticipation. Momma and I were "window shopping," passing the time together as daddy was working. We had nothing more pressing to do this day and an excursion to see the Christmas tree had been our only purpose. Along the way, however, we would stop to admire the holiday decked store windows.

"Oh, momma, look!", I shouted as I pulled her towards a glittering, glistening store front. "Look, just what I've always wanted, in my whole life!"

Momma peered through the window. Sweaters, skirts, blouses and a jumble of accessories were scattered among an array of Christmas ornaments, a formidable Santa and a snow-covered village populated by tiny figurines. 'Martin's' was the newest addition to the town square, a gem of a store occupying a prime corner location in the heart of downtown Hagerstown. It was as yet unvisited by us and we were intrigued by its newness and sparkle.

"What? What have you wanted all of your life?" she questioned as a slow grin appeared on her otherwise solemn face.

"That, that!" I exclaimed as I pointed to a sweater in the far back left corner of the display window. It was a deep blue sweater with two red reindeer, antler to antler, embroidered on the front. Small red **X**s were woven throughout the blue background and red cuffs and neckband completed the design. I had to have that sweater. My whole life depended on that sweater. I would be the envy of my class in that sweater. I would be the warmest child in that sweater. I would be the most popular girl in school in that sweater. I had to have that sweater.

Momma stooped down and squared her face against the glass pane to get a better look at this treasure. She agreed that it was a nice sweater and looked quite warm. It would be an investment towards the snows that would surely come. I could see she was in agreement. The sweater was going to be mine.

I pushed the glass door open in a wide arc and strolled in with momma a few steps behind me. We stood in the middle of the spaciousness, inhaling the perfumed air, gazing at the wondrous displays in awe of a magic world just a few steps away from Potomac Street. There was a quiet hush, an elegance, that permeated the entire room, unlike anything I had ever experienced. I looked at momma. She gazed back and whispered, “What are we doing here?”

It was too late to retreat. A well-groomed, elegant lady quickly approached us. “May I help you?” she asked, a slow glance expertly evaluating us from head to toe.

I straightened up to my full height and cleared my throat in an effort to find my voice. Before I could state our mission, momma quickly responded. “Yes,” she said in a sophisticated tone I had never heard before. “The sweater in the window, please. The blue one. With the red reindeer.”

“Yes, Madame,” the sales clerk replied. “This way, please.”

She walked in front of us, hips swishing from side to side, perfume billowing out towards us, high heels sinking into the thick carpeting. We came to a small room and she turned to face us. “Please have a seat,” she said, gesturing towards two velveteen-covered chairs. Momma and I gracefully deposited ourselves onto the waiting chairs as the saleslady disappeared behind a velvet-curtained doorway. I hid my scuffed saddle shoes under the chair as momma straightened the hem of her coat to cover the worn cotton dress beneath.

The velvet curtains parted as the saleslady reappeared with a stack of sweaters in her arms. The blue sweater with the red reindeer was on top of the stack and I could barely contain my excitement. “That's the one,” I whispered to momma; “that's the one.”

Momma nodded and asked the saleslady if she could see the reindeer sweater. “Of course, Madame,” she replied, handing the coveted sweater to momma.

Momma unfolded the sweater and shook it briskly to remove the creases. She eyed it from top to bottom, side to side, front to back. “Hmmmm,” I heard her mutter as she pondered the merits of the sweater. Clothing was not purchased hurriedly or haphazardly or on a whim. Clothing had to be inspected and evaluated as to practicality, longevity, investment and weariblity. “Hmmmm,” she mumbled.

“Stella, stand up,” momma commanded. I jumped from the velveteen chair and stood before her. Surely momma was as enraptured by the sweater as much as I. Surely she would buy it for me, her one and only child. Momma placed the sweater gently across my chest, pulling the shoulders in place, measuring the arm length, testing the knitted waistband. She twirled me around and placed the sweater across my back, measuring every inch up, down and across. “Hmmmmm.”

The saleslady impatiently tapped her foot against the carpeted floor. She coughed quietly a few times, bringing our attention back to the reality of the moment. “Has Madame made her choice?” she asked. “It is a very beautiful sweater for a very beautiful young lady” she said, a forced smile slicing across her heavily made-up face. “Yes, a very beautiful sweater.”

Momma gently folded the sweater and placed it back on the stack of sweaters. “How much is this sweater?” she asked in a quiet voice, eyes downcast, avoiding the steady gaze of the saleslady. I squeezed momma's hand to convey a message of how badly I needed that sweater.

“Madame, the sweater is a bargain at twelve dollars.” She picked up the sweater in anticipation of wrapping it. She began folding it, layering soft, pale pink tissue between the folds. I followed her every move, hardly daring to breathe. I envisioned placing the pink tissue in my dresser drawer and gently depositing the sweater within its folds. I saw myself strutting into my classroom on Monday, the new sweater proudly displayed.

"Twelve dollars?" questioned momma. "Twelve dollars; is that correct?" I sensed a problem. I looked at her and silently mouthed, "twelve dollars."

She looked away from me. She pointed to the sweater, focusing her gaze on the saleslady. "I don't think it is quite what we are looking for. It is a nice sweater but I think a plain sweater would be a better one, more practical, one without all those patterns. Thank you for your help."

Momma gently took my hand and pulled me through the store, out the gleaming glass doors and back onto Potomac Street. The glittering lights seemed duller; the gaiety had disappeared; the tree looked sorrowful. There was no joy for me for there was to be no reindeer sweater. Momma glanced down at me and gently placed her arm around me and pulled me closer. "Come on, let's go see daddy at the restaurant. We'll have a hot chocolate. Doesn't that sound good?"

I bit my lip to squelch a sob. Tears trickled down my cheeks. I tugged at my sweater, the hated orange and brown sweater, the sweater that would have to see me through one more winter. I wiped my tears on the sleeve of the hated sweater, gulped back a sob and quickly slipped my hand into momma's waiting hand.

"Okay," I said; "okay."

I was about 12 when we moved to the "suburbs" to a nice brick house with a large yard. There were many youngsters my age and friendships were made easily and quickly. We soon were the Mealey Parkway Gang - we had our secret club, we had our summer lemonade stands and our winter snowball battles. We were a loyal group and undaunted in our search for togetherness.

THE HIDEOUT

We stood there, the five of us, staring down into the deep crater we had just finished digging. Dick T., Dick R., and Dick S. had performed the manual labor. Jackie and I, the "weaker sex," provided the encouragement - and the lemonade. It was done. All we had left to do was sculpt out the interior. The clubhouse was almost a reality.

Dick T., being the tallest, jumped into the crater to check the dimensions. Was it deep enough? Was it wide enough? He peered above the edge and declared it suitable for occupancy. We were ready for the interior design.

Two rooms soon emerged, joined by a narrow tunnel. We gouged out "shelves" in the walls for candles, the better to see with, and placed discarded carpet remnants, a recent find, on the floor for a touch of luxury. This was to be the finest clubhouse in existence. We brought in supplies of candy bars and Cracker Jacks. We were finally operational.

Rules were soon established and officers elected. We were sworn to secrecy and promises of lifelong friendship were pledged with clasped hands and the club chant. We were the omnipotent Mealey Parkway gang.

We met once a week. We trudged through the field and crossed the little stream. We uncovered the opening, cleverly concealed with an old cotton rag rug. We jumped down, one by one, and stood shoulder to shoulder in the cramped confines of our clubhouse. We were invincible, this Mealey Parkway gang.

****

NOTE: Looking back, how did we escape suffocation? The possibility of a cave-in at any moment was there. The likelihood of injury was always prevalent and we had not a clue. Our parents had no idea where we were. The reality of what could have happened still frightens me. But we were the omnipotent five, proof positive that God surely looks after children and fools.

Soon digging in dirt lost its luster. Junior High School was a turning point. Boys became the focus of our attention at Woodland Way Junior High School and though we knew not what we were doing, flirting was rampant. Current fashion was studied, hairdos were perfected and targets of our affection were marked.

Y DANCE

Dating was not yet something we did. But Friday night dances at the YMCA were the social highlight of our existence. The girls would gather on one side of the room and the boys clustered on the other. Nervous smiles were exchanged but no one dared make a move.

Slowly, girls would begin dancing with girls as the scratchy recorded music beat out the tempo. We suffered through the steps together, hoping a brave young boy would tap our shoulder and cut-in. And sometimes they did. It was awful but we endured it week after week.

Gradually, as the weeks went by, the boys became bolder and would cut in, taking the girl of their choice to twirl around the dance floor as the other girl made her way back to the chairs lined up against the wall. Rejection was cruel but we lived for Friday night at the Y as the social outlet for us. We loved dancing with the boys and still not knowing what we were doing, we innocently began the formation of "impure thoughts."

I remember one evening when Buddy asked if I would like to go with him for a soda after the dance..Silent panic set in, for I knew I could not do this. But how could I turn him down and still keep the interest burning? I told him my father was to pick me up after the dance. This was not unusual then, for we either walked, rode the bus or parents provided transportation. "Call your dad," Buddy said, "and tell him you'll be home later. I'll walk you home."

Sheer panic. "I can't call him, I don't have any change for the pay phone."

"No problem," he said as he graciously handed me the coin and walked me to the nearby public phone booth.

While he watched, I pretended to place the coin in the proper slot and dialed random numbers. After a reasonable wait, I began my imaginary conversation with what I hoped Buddy would believe was my father. I shook my head, rolled my eyes and made gestures to Buddy as he stood outside the phone booth, illustrating how badly my conversation was going. I slammed the phone down, opened the phone booth and stepped out to the waiting Buddy.

"Gosh, Buddy," I said, "my dad insists on picking me up. We have to go to Waynesboro to pick up my mom from a friend's house. He said no." I pouted and looked up at him with my most beguiling smile. "Next time, maybe?"

I knew there would not be a next time, for "nice Greek girls" did not go out for sodas with boys.

The final years of junior high school and the first two years of high school are a blur. I have faint memories of good friends, good times, basketball games where we cheered ourselves hoarse, and, of course, the Y dances. Somehow I circumvented my restrictions and pursued a happy social life and academic recognition. I excelled in both. High school then presented its own brand of challenges.

FIRST DANCE, LAST DANCE

"I'm going!", I screamed. "I'm going and I don't care!"

The Junior-Senior Prom was just weeks away and I was determined to be there. I had endured high school freshman and sophomore years with casual parties and group gatherings, but single dating was still not that prevalent. No one had cars or much money. Our social life was limited to school functions, football and basketball games and the daily after-school gatherings at the "Valencia Soda Shop" across the street for sodas and conversation. There was no peer pressure as to who was more popular, for we were all in the same situation. The Junior-Senior Prom, however, was the highlight of the season, the culmination of the junior year of high school. I had to go.

"Stella, what am I going to tell your father?"

"Tell him we are going in a group and that it is important for me to go."

"I'll do my best," my mother responded.

"Will you make me a dress?" I asked.

I left the difficult task of convincing my father to my mother as I pondered other more important issues, such as, who to ask to the prom.

I had a secret crush on Frankie, the basketball star at St. Mary's Catholic School. Somehow, my friends and I had started "hanging out" at the drugstore in the heart of town rather than the "Valencia," the Hagerstown High School hangout. We were intrigued by the Catholic boys and Frankie was especially tempting. Dark hair, smoldering brown eyes, an Italian charmer and a great basketball player, no less. He,I decided, would be my escort to the prom. Despite the fact that other than idle chatter at the soda fountain, I had no other encounters with Frankie, but the secret crush I had on him made him even more irresistible.

Two weeks before the prom, I bumped into Frankie and Phil at a concert at the high school. “Hi, Phil, Frankie,” I said as I sidled up to Frankie’s side. “Wasn’t that a good concert?” I asked.

Silence.

“Uhhh, Frankie, uhhh…” I stammered. “What are you doing June 6? Can you go to the prom with me?”

“Uhhh, yeah, okay. Let me know details, okay?”

And that was how it was done.

Meanwhile, my mother was making me the prom dress and my father was not speaking to me.

Prom night and I was in tears. I had eaten dinner with my parents, all the while trying to convince my father that it was just a dance at the high school just two blocks away. We were going in a group. I would be home early. I was doing nothing wrong. My pleas were met with silence.

The doorbell rang and there was Frankie and the two other couples who were going with us. I had just finished wiping my tears and blowing my nose as I hurried to the door. I ushered them into the living room, dashed back to the kitchen to say goodbye to my parents. They did not come out to meet my friends. They did not wish me a fun evening. Nice Greek girls did not go to proms.

School was over and I was looking forward to a summer of fun before beginning senior year. In July, my parents stunned me with the news that we were moving to Savannah, Georgia. I was devastated. This was to be my graduation year, graduation with my friends. How could I start a new school in senior year? It was cruel, but I had no say. We moved to Savannah, Georgia.

SAVANNAH, GEORGIA
1949 - 1962

Savannah, Georgia was not too accepting of us in the beginning. We were "northerners" and had to earn our place in the Southern social strata. It was hard to make friends at first but I joined the Greek church choir, joined the church youth groups and established my social circle. I even managed to have a wonderful senior year at Savannah High School and even went to the Senior Prom (with a nice Greek boy!).

All too soon carefree childhood came to an end and harsh reality forced me into a life I had never dreamed would be mine.

REALITY

By definition, my father's death was the end of his life. By reality, it was the end of my life as I had known it.

I was 19 years old when my father died. We had been in Savannah, Georgia, almost two years when he died. I was balancing on the threshold of adulthood, but tenuously clutching at the strings of carefree youth, afraid to let go, afraid to step over the divide. The death of my father catapulted me, ready or not, into the arena of adult responsibility. I was only 19 and I didn't want to confront adulthood in such a harsh and hurried way.

I vaguely remember the funeral service. I was overcome by the ritual of the service, the overpowering incense, the droning chanting, the finality of it all. I remember the houseful of friends and sympathizers, all with good intentions to comfort us and help us forget. I hated them. I hated their being there. I sat next to my mother, staring at them, sending mental messages to them to leave. They meant well, I told myself, but God! I wanted them out of there. I wanted to scream. I wanted to seclude myself away from their cloying, well-meaning words of comfort and self-conscious smiles of sympathy.

The door finally closed on the last mourner and I was alone with my mother. She silently retreated into her room and I into mine, neither of us able to console the other, only able to fall into the abyss of our individual grief and mourning.

The rain came in torrents that night. Trees swished back and forth, dragging their wayward branches across my bedroom windows. I muffled my cries under my pillow. My mind traveled the distance to Bonaventure Cemetery. I saw rain splattering on the newly-dug grave, mudpuddles forming and my father alone in this so-called place of peace and comfort. I cried relentlessly.

Dawn came and with it the reality of life as it would now be. We were alone, my mother and I. No husband or father. Alone. I slowly approached my mother as she sat at the kitchen table. I touched her shoulder and cautiously gave her a hug. Ours wasn't a demonstrative relationship. I loved her, she loved me, but hugs had not been easily dispensed between us. She had always been the disciplinarian. My hugs had been reserved for my father. "What do you want now?" he would always ask in his gruffest voice as I crept up behind him, surprising him with a hug. I would see a grin emerge and I would just hug a little harder.

1949
left to right- Stella, Dad, Mom
Easter, 1949 in Reading, Pa.

Our last photo taken together, 1949. We had gone to Reading, PA, to celebrate Easter there all together for the last time before moving to Savannah, GA.

My mother coughed. She sighed. I gently hugged her again and shared her pain. She looked so small, so forlorn, fragile and vulnerable. She knew that despite her infinite wisdom and knowledge of so many things, she now had to rely on me. Limited knowledge of the English language, ignorance of life beyond family and home had isolated her and left her with no other choice. She was still the "lady of the house" but I was now "head of household."

And I was only 19.

I picked up the pieces and made a life for myself and my mother. After all, I was my mother's child and it was my duty to take care of her. I never questioned, I never lamented "why me?". It was what life had dealt me and I had to make the most of it. I got a job, I assumed responsibilities way beyond my years and made a life for us....just another "nice Greek Girl" doing what she had to do.

My mother always encouraged me to join my friends and enjoy my life, telling me her life was now over, but mine was ahead of me. I was eager to work, save money and live life. I had witnessed first-hand that life had to be lived one day at a time. Being part of the Greek youth in Savannah, Georgia, was the best thing that could have happened to me at that point of my life. Church and church youth activities gave me the opportunity to have fun, travel and make new friends within the safe confines of our religion and ethnic boundaries. We had wonderful times and always felt safe. Some of the more interesting adventures I now share with you.

SUNRISE

Forty days of Lent had finally come to an end. The Easter Resurrection Service was celebrated with a midnight liturgy. Hours of a beautiful service reinforced our faith and the chanting, incense and lilting voices of the choir (mine included) elevated us to another dimension. It was the culmination of a long period of fasting, church services and limited socialization and we were secretly glad it was now over.

We eagerly awaited the traditional Easter "magiritsa"(a hearty meal centered around the customary Easter soup and roast lamb) gathering in the church hall following the midnight service. This was a community meal that brought young and old alike together to break the fast, break bread and a few red Easter eggs, as custom dictated. We couldn't wait.

At the conclusion of the service, with the final notes of "Christos Anesti" (Christ is Risen) echoing in the empty chambers of the church, we ripped off choir robes and angelic white collars and made our way to the church hall, surreptitiously eyeing the many new Easter outfits on display. This was a fashion show in progress. We were friends, but we were in competition also as to who would have the "sharpest" (the word of that era) outfit.

Following the meal, pent up energy was high and we were not ready to go home with parents. Nothing was open at that hour of the morning - by now, it was 4 a.m. We didn't dare suggest a party at anyone's home, knowing it would be vetoed by the mothers, as they all would be facing a day of cooking for the family Easter dinner. What to do?

"Hey, let's go to the beach!" someone shouted.

"Yeah, great idea!" we responded.

We rushed home, grabbed bathing suits, towels and sandals and regrouped for the caravan to the beach. Parents had not had time to say "yea"or "nay", as we were in and out of our houses in record time and chugging the few miles to the beach before they realized what was happening.

6 a.m. and the beach was serene. No clutter, no people, just the sand, water and few remaining stars. We threw our towels on the sand and secured our space for a few hours of much-needed sleep. It was heavenly.

Hours later, we swam, jumped the waves, sunned ourselves, walked and played the inevitable game of handball. We felt so free, so close to nature, to each other and to God. We made it home just in time to join our families for dinner. It was the best Easter we had ever had.

Of course, there was "talk" about our night at the beach. We were "the wild ones", the "older" ones, the "uncontrollable ones." The teenagers a few years behind us were shocked by our "all-nighter" but secretly, I'm sure, were planning their Easter Sunrise service when they, too, would be of age.

NASSAU IS "MO' BETTAH"

We were young and adventurous and we were going on our first cruise to the islands. Marina, Helen, Alice and I had talked of nothing else for weeks. Our days had been filled with the mandatory pre-cruise shopping sprees, requisite diets to slenderize ourselves into emaciation, new hairstyles to be tried and retried, and balancing check books to assure adequate funds. The excitement had exceeded all boundaries.

Our parents, on the other hand, had not been too enthusiastic. They were hesitant to let us go into the unknown, beyond easy reach of a telephone. We played our trump card by inviting Pina to join us on the trip. She was older; she was wiser; she was of sound mind and body; she would be our chaperone. The scheme worked. Our parents breathed a sigh of relief knowing Pina would not let us stray. Pina innocently looked forward to a pleasant holiday. We prided ourselves in the conspiracy.

It was time to begin the trip. We waited patiently in line to board. The ramp from the dock to the ship deck swayed gently back and forth, a soft breeze blowing around us as we inched our way up. We hung onto the sides for safety, not daring to look at the swirling water below. One by one, we reached the safety of the deck. We stood against the brass railing, leaning out as far as gravity would safely allow, waiting for the ship to set sail.

The "Bahama Star" slowly pulled away from the Miami dock, churning the blue water below, sending swirls of white caps everywhere. Confetti cascaded downward, swirls of red, blue, green and yellow dots enveloped us, obscuring the view. Horns blasted. Passengers shouted farewells, frantically waving to family and friends below. The excitement of the confetti, the hornblowing and the shouting energized us and we were primed for the adventures that were sure to come. We were on our way to Nassau.

I stood there, hair blowing wildly in the breeze, watching seagulls as they screeched and soared. I watched the coastline slowly disappear as we sailed away from work, routines, family and telephones.

Suddenly, I noticed someone approaching our group. He was tall; he was handsome; he was wearing a white uniform and he was stopping in front of us. He glanced at the five of us and smiled a shy smile, white teeth flashing in his suntanned face. We waited. He looked at me and said, "Hello, Chinese."

I stared, studying every feature of his face, trying to bring up a memory from the recesses of my mind. Suddenly, I knew. It was John, a crew member from the Greek freighter "Industrious," a ship that had limped into the Savannah harbor several years ago for repairs. What was he doing here? I turned to Helen, Alice, Marina and Pina and in awe informed them that this was John from the "Industrious"....did they remember? We re-introduced ourselves to him. We shrieked, we laughed, we dredged up memories of the months the "Industrious" had remained in Savannah and the many parties, dances and dinners that we had all shared with John and other members of the crew.

With the passage of time, of course, John had forgotten my name, but he remembered my face and recalled naming me "Chinese" while in Savannah. At the time, he thought I looked very oriental and the nickname "Chinese" became his name for me. Eventually tiring of the constant kidding, I had confided in him, with great sincerity, that absolutely, yes indeed, I was Chinese. My mother, I told him, was Chinese and my father was Greek. He believed me and the nickname stuck. Now, years later, here he was, a First Captain on the "Bahama Star." He said he remembered all of us from his days in Savannah and was eager to talk; however, special glances were being sent in Alice's direction, glances that spoke of many things.

He quickly told us the crew was not allowed to socialize with passengers outside the boundaries of their assignments. However, he hastily added in a low whisper, the majority of the crew was Greek and he would make plans for all of us to meet, if we would like. With that closing message, he turned and left to attend to the many duties his position demanded. Thirty minutes out to sea and we were already involved in intrigue.

We descended into the bowels of the ship to find our room and our luggage. We were on the fourth deck, all that five struggling, working girls could afford. The room consisted of six bunk beds and a sink. Showers and bathrooms were located down the passageway and had to be shared with other passengers on our deck. In order to make room to stand or move about in our room, all the luggage was piled onto the sixth bunk. We each chose our respective bunks, realizing that we would have to climb in and out, one at a time, to get dressed and out before the next one could venture forth. Youth has a way of surviving even the harshest of surroundings and we were fearless.

We headed for the showers. There were two stalls, one for men and one for women. We had to wait our turn as others had formed a line before us. Helen and I were the last two in line and I was growing quite impatient. I wanted to be showered, dressed and up on the deck, pronto! Helen finally reached the door to the women's shower stall. As she entered the cubicle, I jumped into the men's shower stall, determined to be in and out before anyone could discover my transgression. I showered with great trepidation, fearful of discovery, but more concerned with what awaited us on the upper deck.

Back in the cabin, we took turns dressing, four of us sitting in our respective bunks while the fifth dressed. We finished in record-breaking time and began our ascent to the first deck for the Captain's Welcoming Reception before going to dinner.

The reception was in full swing and we waited in line to be properly introduced to the Captain and his officers. A festive mood prevailed and we soon realized a cruise was non-stop fun and entertainment. We went from deck to deck, from lounge to lounge, feasting on fabulous food, sipping exotic tropical drinks and dancing to native rhythms. We were having a wonderful time and this was just Day One. What more could there possibly be?

John paused at our table during the dinner hour. He introduced himself to all the diners at the table, welcoming everyone aboard. He surreptitiously slipped a note to Alice and quickly walked on to the other tables, greeting everyone, inviting them to participate in the many activities. Alice quickly ripped the envelope open and read the note to us. It was an invitation for the five of us to meet in his quarters at 8:30 p.m. He mentioned that he had invited some of the other Greek crew members to join us there so that we could plan our agenda for the three-day stopover in Nassau. Alice passed the invitation around and we assured ourselves that it was all very legitimate, correct and proper. Pina looked somewhat skeptical but we soon convinced her that it was going to be fun and that it was okay, really it was!

Dinner was finished and dishes cleared away. We made our way to the upper deck to enjoy the last remnants of the day. Calypso music was playing, people were swaying and tropical drinks were flowing as we descended to the second deck. We were now in restricted territory, the crew's quarters, and we hurriedly made our way to John's cabin. Alice knocked timidly and the door swung open almost immediately. We were ushered in and were impressed by the comfort and space. Compared to our fourth-deck "crater" this was luxury at its finest. John graciously offered us a choice of drinks and snacks, all accompanied by the latest Greek ballads on the stereo. Introductions to the other crew members followed. Some were from Greece, and others were American. We clicked immediately and it was evident this was going to be a fun cruise. Most of the passengers were honeymooners, which limited our establishing any social relationships. The friendship with the crew, therefore, would afford us companionship that we had not expected. Plans were quickly made for going to the beach after we docked the next morning, and visits to the local calypso clubs would take place that evening. Ringside seats would be arranged for us by John at the "Cat and the Fiddle," the best of all the local limbo clubs.

Next morning, bright and early, the "Bahama Star" slipped quietly into its dockside berth. The sounds of music and local dialects overtook us as we watched native youngsters climb aboard, standing on the ship's railing, diving into the deep, calm water below for coins. The larger the coin, the deeper it seemed to go and it was breathtaking waiting for the young divers to surface, triumphantly waving the coins retrieved. The lilting accent of the natives was intoxicating and we felt so far removed from our ordinary lives in Savannah, Georgia. Shouts of "Hey, mon, ova' heah," beckoned passengers to toss all their excess change into the swirling water. Torrents of coins floated downwards, droves of youngsters propelled upwards out of the churning water, wildly jubilant with their recoveries. The sing-song chanting of "Nassau is mo' bettah!" accompanied our every step and became our mantra.

The ship was firmly anchored and securely docked. We were free to enjoy Nassau for three days, returning to the ship only for dinner and as our hotel every evening. As planned, we met John and his friends and chugged our way to the beach on a crowded water taxi, eager to soak up the island sun. The beach was beautiful and the water was so deep, so clear, an astonishing aqua blue; a color so unbelievable I wanted to bottle it up and take it home with me. We romped, swam, sunned, walked the beach, gathered exotic shells. We laughed, we talked and shared tidbits of our lives with newfound friends.

It was soon evident we were breaking up into "couples". Alice was spending her time with John. Helen was with Bob. Marina with Jim. Tassos was with me. Our long-awaited shipboard romances were being launched. Although Alice and Helen had the more "serious" relationships developing (with their own stories to tell), we were all together as a special circle of friends. It was an exciting, intoxicating time and with broken romances to forget and new friendships to be encouraged, it was an adventure waiting for us and us alone.

I had the added indulgence of having Chico as a dedicated admirer. Little Chico was the native busboy serving our table. He had appointed himself as my personal escort whenever he could. I didn't want to encourage him, but didn't want to offend him either …. what to do? So, in every picture taken on the ship, Chico is standing right next to me, red jacket ablaze with gold buttons, grinning from ear to ear.

We partied on the ship, we partied in the local clubs, we partied anywhere and everywhere. We were soon labeled the "fun group" of the ship. One night found us teaching passengers how to Greek dance. The band played their version of the Greek rhythms and we turned, whirled, circled and waved the handkerchiefs, lost in our exuberance and had everyone clapping for more. We were truly the "stars" of the "Bahama Star."

We eventually met some of the Nassau Greek young people through John and they, too, became a part of the "fun group." I became enamored with Charlie, whose family owned the local department store. Frequent shopping trips provided me opportunities to chat with him, ensuring that he would be a part of the group for each evening's adventures. The laughs, the fun, the learning how to "meringue" and "limbo," swimming, shopping, eating, drinking, sightseeing and dancing filled our days and nights. It was a wonderful time for the five of us to be young, to be free, to be having fun and even savoring a shipboard romance or two.

All too soon, it was time for the "Bahama Star" to turn and wend its way homeward, back to Miami. The strains of "meringue" and "limbo" music drifted from the island toward us as our ship sailed away. The crew assumed their formal duty status and we joined our dining companions for the last evening at sea. Chico served our dinners and smiled longingly at us. Bob grinned at Helen from a distance and as John walked by, he quickly winked at Alice and glancing at each of us murmured under his breath, "Nassau is mo' bettah." We nodded in unison and began the journey home.

left to right- Alice, Stella, Helen, Pina, Marina

The following experience is one that I still relate to people and one that brings forth envious "Oh's" and "Ah's." Helen, Alice and I still remember our encounter with stardom.

TWO LETTERS AND A PICTURE POST CARD

He came; he saw; he conquered. This is how I met Telly Savalas.

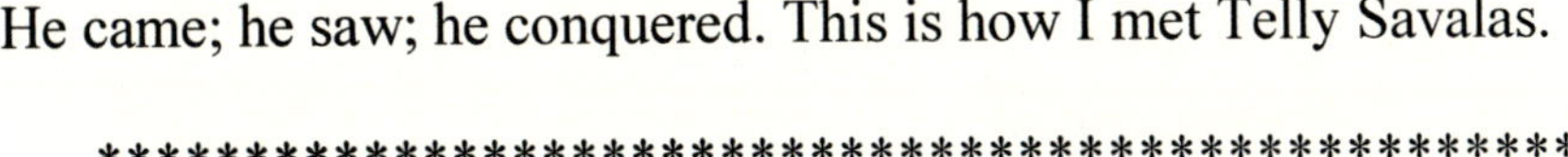

Summer, 1961. Life was slow and easy. And one day, the cast and crew of "Cape Fear" arrived in Savannah, Georgia, and life was never the same again.

It was a Friday evening and Helen, Alice and I were heading for the movie, topping off a busy work week with some much-needed amusement. En route, Helen and Alice excitedly told me about the movie-making that was to take place in Savannah, stressing that ROBERT MITCHUM was starring in the film. "And," continued Helen, "Gregory Peck! and Polly Bergen!..." As our excitement grew, strategies were quickly contrived as to how we could best catch a glimpse of these famous Hollywood stars. Imagine, Bob and Greg and Polly would be living among us for weeks!

Alice turned to me, her big brown eyes filled with star-struck wonder and related additional news. "Telly Savalas is here, too." Helen looked as if she knew what Alice was talking about, but I hadn't a clue.

"Who's he?", I asked.

"I don't know," she replied, "but he's in the movie, too.....And......I think he's Greek! Savalas sure sounds like it, don't you think?" We pondered over this fact. It could well be, but we were more interested in meeting Robert Mitchum.

As agreed, we met the next morning, Saturday, by Armstrong Junior College where the first day of filming was being set up. Barriers separated the area from the many bystanders, but Helen, Alice and I had found each other quickly and claimed our space to view the intricacies of film making. "There he is, there he is," Helen screamed, pointing wildly in the direction of a nearby trailer set up on the college grounds. Stepping out was none other than Robert Mitchum. A unified gasp went up from the crowd as he randomly glanced around, his deep, brooding, drooping eyes picking out the most attractive of the female species in the crowd. His lanky hair fell in his eyes, the cigarette dangled from his mouth. He sneered and sauntered towards the chalk lines drawn for the scene to be filmed, and we three believed he had really looked at us. At us!

Sightings of Gregory Peck and Polly Bergen took place as the scene unfolded. Gregory was so tall, so solemn and handsome. Polly was gorgeous, and her eyes - a startling blue - were incredible. She exuded friendliness and we shyly waved whenever she glanced our way.

Being young and restless, we soon tired of the same scene being shot over and over and over. How tedious; nothing as we had envisioned movie making to be. We moved on, fighting our way through the crowd and rounded the corner. Another scene was being prepared for later filming and as we watched the preparations being made, we wondered if any other "famous people" were there for us to recognize and be impressed by. Alice spotted a tall figure leaning against the iron fence. She whispered, "I think that's Telly Savalas." We looked and we liked what we saw. If this was Telly, and if he was Greek, we had to talk to him, offer our blend of Southern and Greek hospitality, for to do less would be most unfriendly.

"Alice," I said, "as president of our youth group, you should introduce yourself …and…and…. and invite him to the dance next Saturday night!"

"Yeah," seconded Helen, "why not?"

Alice looked at the imposing figure still leaning on the fence and said, "Not me; no way!" Alice, the most gregarious of us all, with a fantastic sense of humor, the logical one to approach him in her capacity of "president", was freezing up on us. We stood there, staring, wishing, wanting and not moving.

"I'll do it," I announced suddenly and before timidity overtook me, I sprinted into the courtyard and marched directly up to this mystery man. He was looking in the opposite direction and did not see me as I approached. I stood up as tall as I could in my ballet slippers, the latest fashion trend, and tapped him on the shoulder. "Excuse me," I said with more bravado than I really felt; "excuse me, but are you Telly Savalas?"

"Yes," came the gruff reply and he stared directly into my eyes, never flinching.

"Are you Greek?", came my next question.

"I am; why?", he challenged.

"Well, Mr. Savalas, my friends and I are Greek and…"

With that, he said, "Call me Telly!" and he reverted instantly into Greek. "Lepon, yati then melame Elinika?" ("Well, then, why aren't we speaking Greek?") He began, the melodious Greek words tumbling from his mouth. I was so excited; I was so electrified; I was so in love!

By now, Alice and Helen had slowly inched their way into the courtyard and were standing slightly to the right of me. I turned and in my most gracious manner proceeded to introduce Telly to them. He was an electrifying personality and soon had us mesmerized. We were star-struck and he wasn't even a star yet. He was amusing, he was gracious, and he was taking the time to chat with three slightly dazed young females.

"Stage three, Savalas," boomed out a voice. He waved his hand in acknowledgment and picked up a script lying on the ground by a tree.

"Gotta go, ladies; sorry….but come back tomorrow and I'll make sure you have front row space to watch, okay?" We nodded mutely in unison, watching him saunter inside the building. As soon as he had disappeared, our pent-up excitement and enthusiasm burst forth in a babble of sound….What to wear tomorrow? What time to meet? How could we get to know more about Telly? Could/should/would we invite him to our dance next Saturday? We were in a state of total chaos.

It took forever for tomorrow to dawn, but finally tomorrow became today and we were ready for our adventure with Hollywood. Helen, Alice and I met at the designated rendezvous spot and fought our way to the front of the crowd, pressing against the wooden sawhorses forming the barrier between "us" and "them." We were undaunted, however, for hadn't Telly said he would make certain we were given a prized viewing spot? Surely, he hadn't forgotten. We stood there, shifting from foot to foot, eager to spot him. Our stomachs growled, breakfast having been forgotten. The heat of the early morning sun began to bake us.

Telly walked briskly out from his trailer and we began waving. Our movements soon caught his eye and he walked directly towards us. We stood there in stunned silence not believing he had actually meant what he had said.

"Kali mera," ("Good morning) he began and we parroted back, "Kali mera." He made us follow him a few steps and pointed to an area marked off with heavy ropes. "Stand back in there," he said. "Filming starts in about 10 minutes and I'll look for you again later." With that, he took off for the set. We turned to each other and just grinned. We were special guests of Telly Savalas! We could feel the stares of those around us, wondering who we were. We basked in our glory.

Making movies was not exciting. It was tedious, tiring and even boring. But we dared not leave; we dared not lose sight of our idol. We took turns running out for food and drink and finding nearby bathrooms. Soon, the day's filming was over. Telly found us and told us to return again the next day. We thanked him profusely and started the trip back home, wondering how poor Telly was going to spend his evening in a lonely hotel room.

Next afternoon, we were again in our reserved spot. We had decided that we needed to plot something more than just watching him from a distance. We had to talk to him; we had to invite him to our dance. This was now Monday and the dance was five days away. There was no time to waste. "I know," I said, "I'll ask him for an interview for the church community bulletin; then, we can ask him to the dance!"

Telly managed to take a break halfway through filming and stood by us for a few minutes. With my heart pounding wildly within my rib cage, I asked if he could possibly grant us an interview - for the church and for the community. He grinned and said, "Sure; why not?"

"Well, when?", I persisted.

"Come by about 7 tonight, if okay with you."

Okay? Was it okay? It couldn't be more okay! I summoned all the casualness I had and asked him where. Helen and Alice stood in stunned disbelief. Was this really happening?

"Room 704, DeSoto Hotel," he informed me and waving his hand, swung around for the walk back to the set. "7 o'clock, okay?"

We were in a total frenzy. We were excited; we were frightened; we were challenged. But we were going to go through with it. Adventurous as we may have imagined ourselves to be, we were somewhat unnerved. How were we going to go to a movie star's hotel room, just the three of us? To be on the safe side, we decided to ask Helen's brother, Johnny, our ever stalwart protector, to accompany us to Room 704, DeSoto Hotel.

The door to Room 704 loomed gigantically in front of us. We debated turning around in hasty retreat. But we were determined; we had to go through with this. We knocked on the door. No response. Another knock. We waited. Suddenly the door was flung open and there he was. Our eyes widened. We stared. Telly Savalas was almost naked and all we could do was stand there and look.

He pulled the bath towel tighter around his waist and waved us in. "Come in; come in. I was just finishing my shower. We went way over schedule today....sorry." He opened the door wider, motioning us in. We gazed at the glistening shoulders, the massive chest, the white towel wrapped snugly around his waist as he walked over and plopped down on the white sofa. Was he not going to get dressed? We gazed at him and he gazed at us. What were we doing in a hotel room with a semi-naked movie star? I smoothed my skirt over my knees and demurely crossed my legs at the ankles, as was proper to do. Helen and Alice did the same. We stared at him, trying to keep our eyes from straying too far beyond the towel-wrapped torso.

I cleared my throat and quickly thrust a prepared list of questions at him. With a quivering voice I asked if we could proceed with the interview. He smiled, winked and grabbed the paper from my hand. He scanned the list of questions I had nervously prepared and in two seconds he gave his approval. "Endaxi; (okay); let's begin."

I wrote rapidly as he talked, sometimes keeping to the scripted questions, other times responding to those we threw at him as they occurred to us. We soon forgot his body and focused on his mind. He was brilliant; he was dazzling; he was absolutely splendid.

Interview over, we stood up and headed towards the door, eager to flee but yet reluctant to leave. This was the most exciting event in our lives, collectively and individually. Telly clutched the towel wrap closer to his body and padded across the room to open the door for us. I had to arrange another meeting; I couldn't leave without knowing that I would see him again.

"I can have this ready for you to edit and approve tomorrow. When can we drop it off?", I asked.

"I'll call you," he countered and asked for my phone number. Oh, dear Lord in Heaven, he was going to call me. I gave him my office number.

The next morning, I casually advised the office switchboard operator that I was expecting a call from Telly Savalas, and to find me wherever I was when he called. "Who?", she asked. I informed her and her eyes grew wider and wider as she realized a movie star would have to talk to her before he was able to talk to me. When the call finally came, she put it through to my desk, tore off her headset and ran around the office screaming, "I just talked to a movie star! I talked to a movie star!" No matter that no one knew who Telly Savalas was, movie mania had claimed yet another victim.

"Hello," I said, gripping the telephone.

He said, "This is Telly Savalas, Stella."

"You recognized my voice?", I said and almost stopped breathing.

He said, "How could I ever forget that beautiful voice?" and he gave a low, rumbling chuckle.

"Me?" I squeaked.

He murmured, "How could I forget you, baby?"

I totally lost it. I was a goner. I was really in love. I feigned sophistication and proceeded to tell him of the wonderful interview article I had written and how eager we were to have him approve it. "Call me tonight," he suggested.

"Sure," I replied; "talk to you later," and I shakily replaced the receiver.

I rounded up all the friends I could rally and we headed for the cocktail lounge in the DeSoto Hotel. It was a short walk from the office and I felt safer with friends surrounding me. We entered the dim coolness of the bar, slowly adjusting our eyes to the dark, smoky room. We headed for a corner table, a nice, big, round non-intimate table. We ordered drinks and made idle chatter. We waited for courage. One drink seemed to fortify me and I walked confidently over to the house phone. I dialed "704." Three rings…four rings….and there he was.

"Hi," I chirped; "this is Stella and…."

"I know, baby; I know," he interrupted.

I continued, "We're in the lounge….uh, we're downstairs…uh….uh…..I have your interview ready." I was stuttering; I was making a fool of myself; what would he think of me?

And he said, "I'll be down in five minutes, okay? Ciao, baby!"

I rejoined my friends, plopping down in my chair and wiping my perspiration-soaked hands with the stack of cocktail napkins littering our table. "He's coming….in five minutes!" My heart pounded louder and louder. My ploy had worked. Now, all we had to do was get him to the dance on Saturday.

"Waiter, I'll have another drink, please," I ordered. Five minutes seemed an eternity.

****

The weeks flew by. Telly was by now well ensconced in our community life. Invitations to dances, to the beach, to church, to parties, to dinners, to our homes were issued and none were refused. I basked in my self-righteousness for I had been the one to tap him on the shoulder. I had interviewed him. I had called every time we "just happened" to be in the DeSoto Hotel lounge. I had brought it all about. But now, I had to share him with so many others. He was gracious, witty and his charisma was extraordinary. He was quite the charmer, but sincere with his brand of charm. He made us feel beautiful, glamorous, amusing and sensual. He inspired us to reach greater heights of small-town sophistication. His impact on the three of us especially was colossal.

Filming was now finished. Sets were taken up, props were packed and Telly bid Savannah farewell. Helen, Alice and I were the saddest of all to see him go and I was minus a piece of my heart. He vowed he would return. He said Savannah would be his second home. We promised to write as tears streamed down our faces. We hugged him and shyly kissed his cheek. He was gone.

I could not let it end this way. I made duplicate copies of the many pictures we had taken with him and of him. I relinquished my last copy of the community brochure containing my interview with Telly. I wrote him a letter and packaged it all and sent it on its way to Mr. Telly Savalas, Hollywood, California.

Routine soon returned to Savannah. Work, activities and other responsibilities filled my days. Occasional memories of our meeting with Telly prodded their way into my reality. I often wondered what would have happened had I been less bashful, more aggressive? Temptation had been there, but the "good Greek girl" syndrome had hampered my style. Alas, I was never to have more than my fantasies.

Weeks passed. Summer ended. My days went by and life went on. I was busy but I often wondered where Telly was and what he was doing.

It was now mid-September and a bad head cold found me huddled beneath the blankets, miserable, achy, feverish and cantankerous. To add to my misery, it was raining a hard, steady, wretched rain and gloom was everywhere. I coughed, sneezed and blew my nose all morning. I wanted nothing to eat and nothing to drink. I wanted to be alone with my misery.

The door to my room opened slowly and my mother came timidly into the room. She approached my bed. "Here," she said, "maybe this will make you feel better." She handed me a letter. I did not recognize the handwriting and was about to put it aside for later reading when the return address zoomed out at me…TELLY SAVALAS……could it be real or was I delirious from the fever?

I ripped the envelope open, carefully preserving the return address. The letter tumbled out and I gently unfolded the creases. I read and reread the words, not believing a one of them, but luxuriating in their very being. I threw off the bedcovers; I whirled about the room. A miraculous recovery was in progress.

Settling down, I allowed a few days to go by before carefully composing a letter. My letter was soon on its way to Hollywood and with it, an irrational belief that a response would soon be on its way back to me. Hope sprung eternal, beating its fluttering wings in my heart.

A letter from Budapest arrived one afternoon, its envelope battered and torn. Identity of the sender was obscured and I was curious as to which of my friends was perhaps traveling there. I unfolded the tissue-thin paper and quickly glanced at the words unfurling before me. I turned it over to verify the signature. In bold, black ink strokes, the words leaped out at me. "Love ya, baby….Telly". He hadn't forgotten me, he said. He missed me, he said. He was in Budapest filming for a few months, he said. He'd write again, he said. I clutched the letter and traced the words with my fingers.

"Love ya, baby," I repeated over and over and over…."Love ya, baby."

A picture postcard from Greece eventually arrived with its typical scene of the Parthenon against the brilliant blue Grecian sky. Telly again, the familiar black ink utterances reminding me that he was still thinking of me. His promises to write when he returned to California were sealed with the usual, "Who loves you baby? I love ya, baby."

I waited….and waited.

Two letters and a picture postcard are all that remain.

Telly! (left), me! (right)
1961

Stella — Darling,
I was so surprised
when the photographer
broke in. Forgive
me —

Telly
Savalas
1961

1962 - Present

WASHINGTON, DC

My years in Savannah were a wonderful growing-up time, but it was time to move on. A job offer in Washington, DC was made and I accepted. New friends and new experiences awaited me and I was enthralled with the metropolitan scene and yet felt I would never be able to make my way among so many people and so much traffic. Savannah had felt safe and I was ready to go back. My mother encouraged me to stay and so stay I did.

Eventually, I moved my mother and our household to Washington. It broke my heart to separate her from our home and from her friends, but I had no choice. I had to better my life and she would have to come along for the ride, wherever it was to lead. She made the change slowly but Washington soon became home and Savannah just a memory.

Life offered me many challenges and opportunities and I accepted them in spite of the responsibilities I had been given. I had an exciting career with the FBI and a tour of duty in Paris, France (that can be another book!).

I eventually married, my mother grew older and life became an even greater challenge.

EPILOGUE

LIFE'S LESSONS

The child became the mother.

And the mother became the child.

Following my father's death at age 51, I had assumed the role of wage earner, bill payer and caretaker. The role of "head of household" had been bestowed upon me.

My mother spoke limited English. She had never worked outside the home. Her circle of friends had included women just like herself. They had married and arrived in the United States, leaving their homeland behind, seeking security and a better life. They were to be wife, mother, housekeeper, cook, seamstress, disciplinarian, pastry chef and hostess. Family and home were their responsibility and their greatest achievement.

And so, Greek men worked and Greek women ran the house. Their roles were clearly defined. A wife rarely discussed family finances. She was often ignorant of income and expenses. A weekly allowance was given to her for groceries and incidentals. Through careful planning and clever manipulating, leftover change would be hidden in the recesses of a dresser drawer for future use.

My mother did it all in extraordinary fashion. She ran the household effortlessly. I marveled at her many talents.

I remember well the dresses she created and sewed for me. I remember the delicious meals she prepared three times a day, seven days a week. I remember the many pastries she would bake for the holidays. I remember the daily housecleaning chores with no deviation. I remember watching her hanging laundry out to dry. I remember watching her as she waxed the hardwood floors and scrubbed the kitchen linoleum floor. I marveled at the strength behind the hands beating the many oriental carpets. She was relentless in her efforts to create a clean and harmonious environment for her family.

My father worked long, hard hours at the restaurant in Hagerstown, trying to make a go of his new business venture. Therefore, my mother was the enforcer of rules and the disciplinarian when those rules were broken. She never hesitated to reprimand and punish when necessary. My father was my safe harbor when he was home. I could do no wrong as far as he was concerned and I knew I never wanted to cross that line. And so, my childhood passed.

But life took an unexpected turn. My father died in 1951 after a six-month illness, succumbing to the ravages of lung cancer. My mother and I were left with no knowledge of the future and with no financial resources. The family had moved to Savannah, Georgia, eighteen months before his untimely death. We were still new and in the process of establishing a business, buying a house, making friends and becoming part of the Greek community in Savannah. Eighteen months had not given us time to begin anew and now it was ending.

According to the unwritten script handed out to each Greek daughter, the responsibility of maintaining the household became mine. It was not expected that the grieving widow should find a job. It was not considered acceptable that she remarry. She was to mourn for the rest of her life as the daughter stepped up to fill the role of "head of household."

And so, I became the wage earner and the bill payer. At age nineteen, I assumed responsibilities that many never do. My life was placed on hold so that my mother could live out her life as the weeping widow. Funny, I never resented it; I just accepted it. But now, looking back, I wish I had done things differently.

I lived my life as best I knew how. I got a job and learned how to budget well. I did not feel deprived, but I realize now that I was. I never ached to go to college but now I wish I had. I dated and partied and had fun, but always with a sense of guilt. I did not pursue marriage, opting for short-lived romances. I knew I had a responsibility that was mine alone and should not become a burden for anyone else.

The years rolled by. I had adventures and I had challenges. I was getting older and my mother was getting old - there is a difference. With her fears of aging and the onslaught of the many problems involved with the aging process, she became more and more dependent upon me. She became fearful of losing me, either to a flight from my overwhelming responsibilities, or to marriage or to illness. She hovered and smothered me. She loved me too much and yet not enough to let go, to let me be the person I was waiting to be.

More years went by. Her declining physical and mental health was impacting on mine. I felt as if I lived surrounded by insurmountable walls. I felt as if I carried a burden on my shoulders that I could never put down. I continued to strive for a normal life and busied myself with work and friends. I filled my limited free time with projects and challenges. It was not enough, though. I was becoming unraveled and I knew it.

And then, along came Mike. He was in the throes of a personal anguish of his own. Together we shared our sad stories and found comfort in each other. I discouraged his advances. I wanted only friendship for I felt I could not marry. He persisted and vetoed every reason I gave him as to why I could not marry him. In time, I began to envision a life of my own without neglecting my mother's needs. Perhaps it was possible. Then reality would hit me full in the face and I would despair that it was not.

My mother liked Mike and she encouraged the friendship. She continually invited him to visit and enjoyed a new audience for her old stories. In contrast, though, I could see fear growing in her that I would soon marry and abandon her. On one hand, she lamented that she had been a failure as a mother because I had never married, but on the other hand, subtle acts and remarks indicated to me that she was not willing to let me go.

I felt I was ready for St. Elizabeth's mental institution. I was hanging by a thin thread. I feared for my sanity. I suggested elopement. Mike would not entertain that thought. I wanted to run away from everything and everyone. And so, I was married in the conventional way, in the Greek church, determined that I was going to have a life of my own.

My mother moved into a senior citizens complex and Mike and I commenced our married life in our condominium. It was just a change in scenery for I still had the responsibilities of my mother's care. Every weekend would find me shopping, cooking and cleaning for my mother while my needs were still on hold and I would go home too exhausted to take care of my own home. It was dreadful. But I was a "good Greek girl."

Ten years passed. My mother was retreating more and more within herself. She no longer participated in activities at the complex. No matter what day or what time of day I visited, I would find her lying in bed in the darkened apartment. She was "resting," she would say. It was depressing. I could sense a deterioration in her physical abilities but the mental decline was the most difficult to contend with. Absurb statements, forgetfulness, decline in personal hygiene, fear of eating and refusal of medical care alarmed me. I read every book, attended every lecture, sought every form of assistance. I became an expert on the care of an aging parent.

With no siblings or relatives to help, I had to turn to social workers. They became my family. Many services unknown to me were available for her safety, comfort and well being. Strangers eased the demands on me. I couldn't have done it without them.

The day I had dreaded for years finally came. It was time to find a nursing home facility to take in my mother. Her physical condition had worsened. She was afraid to eat most foods or else she would forget to eat. She was a mere shadow of herself at 91 pounds. She refused to let me bathe her or to wash her hair. It was a battle each time, ending in total frustration and tears for us both. Social Services provided aides to bathe her; she sent them away. "I have a cold, come back tomorrow," she would tell them. Mentally, I saw that she was slipping away from today and hiding in yesteryears. It was frightening to see the woman she had been become the stranger I did not want to know.

The day I took my mother to the nursing home and turned her over to health care professionals was an experience that still tugs at my heartstrings, even after all these years.
She, however, wanted to go and was looking forward to it. She settled into her room and luxuriated in the comfortable bed. I placed her clothes in the closet. I unfolded her bright pink and purple comforter and gave it to her, a familiar reminder of home. She smiled.

It was time for me to leave and I dreaded leaving her within the confines of the nursing home for the first night. I kissed her and told her goodbye. She sat up in bed, eyes wild, confusion written all over her face. "How am I going to cook? Where is my stove? Where are my dishes?" She was lost in the maze of a mind gone blank.

"It's okay, mom; it's okay. They'll cook for you and serve you your meals. You'll see, you'll like it." I patted her and comforted her and tried to allay her fears. I said goodbye and left without looking back. I heard her screaming "Stella….Stella…" I can still hear the echoes of that day.

Slowly the pattern of her days evolved into predictable segments. Time to rise, time to dress, time to eat, time to bathe, time to sleep. She fought routine but couldn't "push any buttons" to get her way. Aides demanded and she relented. I began to breathe a bit easier.

Fantasy overshadowed reality and some of her hallucinations were frightening to me, let alone what she must have been experiencing in her mind. She accused her roommate of being a Russian spy. She described the microphones hidden in shoes and the many clandestine meetings held in her very room with other spies. Where was this coming from, I wondered?

"He raped me," she confessed to me one day. I stared in complete amazement. This shy, sheltered little woman was talking about rape! She accused everyone from my husband to the electricians to fellow residents. What was she reliving, I wondered? Were the years in Adramit, with their constant fear of plundering, pillaging and raping, surfacing from the reservoirs of her mind?

Slowly the bizarre evolved into the more rational. She savored the attention bestowed upon her by the aides and nurses. She thrived on the food and loved being waited on. She glowed with happiness at the attention she was creating and getting. She told many stories about her childhood and her life in America. Some of it was real, much of it was fabricated, but she was happy as she slipped further and further into dementia.

"I'm getting married," she announced one day, shyly showing me her freshly manicured nails painted a bright glowing pink. A lady who had never had a manicure in her life was now flaunting polished nails and looking forward to her wedding. I didn't know whether to laugh or to cry.

"Your father came to see me," she said on another day. "I saw him through the window and he was waving at me." My father had been dead for over 40 years. "That's nice," I said. I was learning.

Sometimes she spoke to me in Greek and other times in English. She knew, however, to speak only in English to the staff. One day she looked at me and wanted to know who I was. That scared me and upset me. Not to be known by your own mother is a difficult thing to endure. "It's me, mom; it's me." She stared at me through blank, unblinking eyes.

Another time she asked, "What's your name?"

"Stella," I answered.

"Ohhhh…I have a daughter; her name is Stella, too."

"Mom, I'm Stella; I'm your daughter; I'm Stella," I repeated, pointing at myself in vain.

She leaned closer and scrutinized my face. “No, not my daughter. You’re a pretty lady but you’re not my daughter. She never visits me.”

I cried.

Eventually all of this became routine and it no longer frightened me. Visits became more and more difficult as conversation became alien. I couldn’t relate to anything she said and she couldn’t comprehend what I was saying. I would sit and hold her hand, hoping that she knew it was I, her daughter, sitting there. And she would lament that her daughter never visited.

Someone had given her a tiny teddy bear. Tan plush, with a ruffled lace collar and skirt, with pearl earrings in its little ears. She would clutch that little bear with all her might, sometimes to ease pain, sometimes to erase loneliness. She wouldn’t part with that bear and I would pretend it was me she was hugging and kissing.

A call at 3 a.m. early one November morning, 1998, roused us from a heavy sleep. “Your mother has taken a turn for the worse. How aggressive do you want us to be?”

This is it, I thought, as I struggled to get dressed in the darkness. We drove to the nursing home as fast as allowed and rushed into her room. She was sleeping soundly and I patted her face and pulled the covers up closer. The nurses briefed me and said it would probably be a matter of time, as her vital signs were not good.

Seven months passed as I watched my mother struggle between life and death. Vital organs were starting to shut down and her body began to bloat. She drifted between wakeful hours and coma-like days. She ballooned to impossible dimensions and I expected her to explode if I even touched her. She never spoke again from that day in November. I would talk to her and caress her and rock the bed to ease her into sleep. I wanted her to know I was there. Me, her daughter,

Stella.

Morphine helped ease her into a calmer state as she continued to swell. Seeping began, or as the aides called it, "weeping." The body was so filled with fluid it was escaping through the pores in her skin. Terry cloth towels were wrapped around her arms to absorb the seeping moisture. Despite all of this and her obvious unawareness of what was happening, she never missed a meal. Breakfast, lunch and dinner were brought to her. With eyes closed, she would open her mouth in anticipation as the aide placed the food in her mouth. She savored every morsel and continued to smack her lips and seek more even after the tray had been removed and returned to the kitchen. How we would smile at her utter contentment.

Memorial Day, Monday, May 1999. I stopped by the nursing home to visit. The aide told me my mother had refused food that morning. A bell went off in my head and I knew this was to be the end. I watched her closely. As usual, there was no utterance of any sound from her. She looked comfortable despite the massive bulk of her body. She drifted in and out of sleep. She refused lunch. She refused dinner as sleep continued to envelop her.

Hours passed. The on-duty nurse finally suggested I go home as there was no visible change or any immediate signs of distress. She sensed my extreme physical, mental and emotional state. She promised she would call if there was any change whatsoever. It would be better for all if I went home, she said.

I was in the shower, luxuriating under the pounding stream of hot water, when the bathroom door opened and I heard Mike calling my name. I knew. He didn't have to say anything; I knew. "They just called from the home," he said. "She's taken a turn for the worse and they advise we get there as soon as possible."

I dried myself off haphazardly and threw on whatever clothes I was able to get my hands on. Mike changed from his bedclothes to jeans and sweater and together we roared down the highway to the nursing home 20 minutes away.

The elevator doors creaked open and we ran up to the nurses' station. I saw my mother's nurse shaking her head from side to side and I dreaded the words I knew I had to hear. "She's gone; you missed her by 10 minutes."

I ran madly down the corridor and into my mother's room. She was lying there in a deep sleep, her face in soft repose. "She's not dead," I screamed, "she's sleeping." I threw myself down on her bed and gathered her into my arms. She was so soft and still so warm. But she was gone.

I lost total control and horrendous sobs racked my body and my tears splashed onto her face. No matter how resigned I thought I had become to this very moment, no matter how much in control I thought I would be, I totally lost it.

"Mom, mom," I screamed, like a lost little girl trying to find her mother. "Mom, mom, don't leave me." I sobbed and hugged her, pressing my body next to hers to warm her and to comfort her.

Mike slowly pulled me away and hugged me. "We have to make arrangements, Stella. We have to talk to the front desk." I followed him down the quiet corridor and quietly asked, "What do I do now?"

The body was wrapped in a clean, soft, pristine white sheet. The body bag was closed over her as I gently pulled the sheet over her face and kissed her one last time. The sound of the zipper of the body bag screeched through the quietness of the room. The gurney was guided out of the room, with the funeral home attendant at one end and Mike at the other. The elevator transported us back to the ground floor and the gurney was guided out to the waiting hearse. I sobbed a goodbye as the gurney was placed in the hearse and the heavy doors slammed shut, enveloping my mother within.

Mike and I walked dejectedly back to the car and began the silent ride home. It was now after 2 a.m. and we were both exhausted and hungry. "Do you want something to eat? Can you eat anything?" he asked. I nodded in the affirmative.

We pulled into the drive-through of a still open McDonald's and ordered our meals to go. Once home, we settled into the kitchen and spread out our McDonald's feast before us. We filled our glasses with Diet Coke, clinked them together and wished my mom God speed.

Losing my mother was so difficult. I still miss here. She became my child and I protected her and tried my best to prevent anything bad happening to her. Eventually, her life ended. I wrote the following to console me in my grief.

DEPARTURE

The day dawned, as had so many before. The sun struggled upwards through the clouds to find its resting spot for the day. Shafts of sunlight slowly filtered through the window as the morning progressed. It was warm, but not unpleasantly so. A soft breeze swayed through the trees and a golden haze settled over the landscape. It was a peaceful May morning.

She awoke at the first kiss of sunlight on her face. She turned her face away from the light, trying to capture a few more minutes of sleep. Today was the day she was to begin a long-awaited trip. She needed her rest for she knew it would be a long journey. She snuggled beneath the soft blue blanket and nestled her head further into the fluffy pillows. She stretched her legs out from their cramped position and sighed as her body found a new spot on the mattress. Just a little bit more of sleep, she wished silently.

It was soon time for breakfast, but she chose not to eat. She was not hungry this morning. Perhaps the excitement of the forthcoming trip was taking precedence; perhaps resting was more important in preparation for the journey. She fell back into a relaxing sleep and with no one to disturb her, dreamt of the trip she was about to take.

The hours crept by. She looked around her, taking in the familiar sights, stamping the images in her memory. Evening slowly descended. The moon replaced the sun. Stars twinkled like a myriad of fireflies swirling and twirling against the black velvet of the sky. The lamp table cast a soft glow, creating gray abstract shadows on the walls. The clock ticked slowly, the second hand making its sweep around the face of the clock, moving the minute hand ahead to the appointed time.

She moved cautiously, careful not to fall. She didn't want anything to postpone this trip. She smiled to herself as she smoothed her rumpled hair into a more presentable appearance. She moistened her lips with her tongue, biting them slightly to give them a rosy glow. It was almost time for the travel escort to arrive.

A knock on the door. "Come in; the door is not locked," she said. Then, a sweep of fresh air blew into the room as the door opened. She looked straight ahead and saw a tall figure standing in the doorway. "Is that you?", she asked. "Is it time to start my trip?"

"Yes, I'm your guide. My name is Luther. Are you ready, or do you need more time?"

"I'm ready," she answered. She took his hand as he helped her walk out of the room. She planted her feet firmly with each step on the hard floor, and clutching his hand, followed him out into the warm night air.

Soon they were flying high above the clouds toward their destination. She had flown many times before but never like this. She remembered the many trips she had taken and the many wonderful memories each trip had created. Somehow, though, she knew that this trip was going to be the trip of a lifetime. She couldn't wait to arrive. There would be so many new sights and many people to meet. She loved adventure and excitement and this was going to be wonderful, she knew.

They descended slowly and came to a halt. She stumbled slightly as she was led towards the exit, anxious and scared as to what awaited her. Luther gently pushed her forward. She grasped the handle and pulled the door open, stepping quickly over the threshold.

ARRIVAL

She felt the excitement, heard the many voices, saw the bright lights and welcoming signs….all for her! “Welcome!” “We’ve Been Waiting For You!”

Music and laughter flowed about her. Hugs and kisses were rained on her. She looked about her, surprised at the many people surrounding her. She had never expected this. This was such a wonderful surprise, a perfect ending to the long trip. And to think she had been hesitant to take this journey. “Why,” she murmured, “this is wonderful; why did I wait so long?”

She soon overcame her shyness and began to rejoice in the reunion. She marveled at the fun and joy all around her and knew she had made the right choice.

But the journey had been a long one. Although she wanted to spend time with the welcoming crowd, she was tired and wanted to rest. “Where do I go now? What do I do?” she asked in a trembling voice. She looked around in search of Luther and found him nearby. She looked up at him, her brown eyes searching his kind face for guidance. She put out her hand, clutching his arm for support.

He slowly guided her forward down the long hallway looming before them. They soon stopped in front of a blue door. “Here you are,” Luther said, “this will be your room for a few days until we process everything.” He opened the door and gently ushered her into a small chamber. “You can rest for a while now,” he said, as he exited and closed the door behind him.

She looked about her, acclimating her eyes to the light. The room was small, but comfortable. There was a bed, a chest of drawers, a small closet, a mirror and a rocking chair. Light came in from the window behind the bed and a skylight in the ceiling. It was a warm, bright, soothing light. It eased away the cold and chills she had; it felt so comforting. She shuffled over to the rocking chair and carefully lowered herself onto the soft cushion. She stretched her legs out before her and gave a push. Slowly the chair rocked back and forth, back and forth. "Ahhhh," she sighed; "ahhh; this is so nice." She rocked and rocked until she fell into a deep, exhausted sleep.

The muffled sound of bells chiming in the distance slowly penetrated her sleep. She opened her eyes and looked about her, uncertain as to where she was and what she was doing there. A sleepy haze still enveloped her and she was frightened. She jumped up quickly, sending the rocking chair into a wild spin. She opened the blue door and looked up and down the empty hallway. There was no one in sight as the bells continued to chime.

She closed the door slowly and stood by the bed, uncertain as to what to do or where to go. She gently touched the quilted comforter on the bed, vaguely remembering a similar colorful pattern of pink and purple flowers. Suddenly she realized it was the same comforter she had used many years ago. How did it get here? Strange, but yet a comforting reminder of home. She opened the closet door and there in wild array were her clothes; clothes she had long outgrown, clothes from her youth. How was she expected to fit in them now? Where were the clothes she had packed? She peeked further into the closet and smelled the sweet aroma of a perfume she had used as a young woman. Pleasant thoughts of yester-years suddenly flooded her bewildered mind. What was happening here?

Turning towards the mirror she was startled to see a stranger reflected there. Who had come into her room? How had they entered? She twirled around to face the intruder and saw no one. She turned back to the mirror and there was the stranger again. She inched closer to the mirror and peered at the image. She felt a pang of recognition. This was not a stranger. She knew this person. Again, she turned to search the room. No one was there.

The room was quiet and flooded with a warm, golden light. Strangely, she felt no fear, only curiosity. She turned towards the mirror again and gazed at the woman staring back at her. She raised her arm and smoothed her hair; the stranger did the same. She blinked; the stranger blinked back. She smiled and a smile was returned. She stepped back and gazed at the image.

She knew this woman. She had been this woman. She was gazing at a thirty-year-old Maria, Maria with the coal black hair cut in a stylish bob. Maria with dark brown eyes ringed with a double row of dark lashes and framed with gently arched eyebrows. Maria as a young stylish matron. How lovely she was.

She looked down at her body. Gone were the wrinkled neck, drooping shoulders and broad hips. In their place a long, slender neck flowed into graceful shoulders. The hips were curvaceous and appealing. She couldn't believe it. She was thirty-years-old again! She took one last look into the mirror to finalize the image and quickly escaped from the confines of her room. She ran down the hallway, singing, her heart pounding wildly, in search of someone to verify her existence.

Maria came to the end of the hallway and stopped before a doorway that loomed before her. It was a dark cherry wood, ornately carved, with a cut-crystal doorknob. She turned the knob slowly and the door creaked open inward. She stepped cautiously into the room as curiosity pulled her inside. She heard voices and laughter as she entered. She found herself in a room filled with many young adults and children of varying ages. As she neared the group, she became aware of familiar faces, faces of long-lost friends. They greeted her happily and smiled at her bewilderment. "Welcome," the shouted in unison.

A young man stood in the far corner, his dark brooding eyes gazing steadily at Maria. She felt the intensity of his stare and slowly turned towards that part of the room. She was drawn to him and mesmerized by his stare. She made her way across the room. Only once before had she felt such magnetism, when she had met Christos, her husband, for the first time. She could not understand the attraction she now felt powerless to fight. Maria stopped before the man and looked at him. She was afraid to say anything, afraid to move forward or turn back. She was rooted there, waiting for him to speak.

"Hello, Maria," he said. "Ive been waiting for you."

"Who are you?" she asked, gazing at features that were becoming familiar. Too familiar. "Christos? It it you, Christos?"

He reached out and pulled her into the warmth of his arms, gently kissing the top of her head. "Yes, it's me," he answered. "I've been so lonely for you. "I'm so happy you are now here."

"But, but.....you're so young, so handsome. I don't understand."

"Maria, Maria," he said, suppressing his amusement. "You are in Heaven now. You are with me and your friends and your sons. We are all here."

She looked at him again and then let her gaze fall slowly on all the other people in the crowded room. Everyone looked young, happy and healthy. No old wrinkled faces, no bent and aching limbs, no helpless invalids. They were vibrant and whole.

She looked at Christos and in bewilderment asked, "How? What has happened to everyone here?"

"Maria," he patiently began, "all adults arrive in Heaven healthy and whole. They become thirty-years-old again, no matter when or how their life on earth ended."

"And the children....what about them?" Maria asked.

"Ahhh.....you know, kids will be kids. They stay the same age as when they arrived and wait for their mommas and pappas to come and take care of them again. Isn't that wonderful?"

"Oh, Christos, I can't believe this. I just want to cry!" and with that, tears began to roll down her face and sobs wracked her body. "I don't know if I should be happy or sad."

"Be happy, Maria. You've had a hard life and have been alone for so long. Now, you are here with us."

"Us?" she asked, "who is us?"

Christos guided her to an area where children and babies of all ages played happily in the sunlight. "There," he said, pointing at a toddler, "there's John. And there, in the cradle, is the twin boy we lost before we could name him. What shall we call him?"

Maria sobbed as she went over to the cradle and gently caressed the sweet baby face looking up at her. She leaned over and kissed him and named him Gregory. "I cried for you every day of my life," she whispered. "I can now rest in peace that I have found you and named you. My sweet baby."

The baby now known as Gregory smiled. His little arms waved wildly in the air, greeting his momma as best he knew how. Maria gently caressed him and tucked the blue blanket carefully around him.

Christos called out to John and the toddler turned to gaze at him. He smiled and gurgled and made his wobbly way over to Christos. "John, this is your momma."

The little one wrapped his chubby arms around Maria's legs, pulling her closer to him as he whispered, "Momma."

Maria could not control the sobs now as she gathered the little boy in her arms. He snuggled his head on her shoulder and caressed her cheek, just as he had so many years ago. "Don't cry, momma," he said; "don't cry," and he began to trace the tears sliding down her face.

Christos gazed at the reunion taking place before him and smiled contentedly. "I'm so happy you are here, Maria. Now, we can ask for a cottage so we can all live together again. It'll take time but time goes by so quickly here."

Maria smiled as images of her happy family flashed before her eyes. Suddenly, she muffled a scream. "But what about our daughter? We've left her all alone."

"Don't worry about her. She'll be fine. Until it is time for her to join us here, I'll ask Luther to watch over her and keep her safe. Does that make you feel better?"

"Yes," murmured Maria. "Luther is a good guardian angel. He watched over me for many years and now he will watch over her. I can be at peace."

Maria walked slowly over to a large window at the end of the room. She gazed out through the mist that whirled outside. She wiped tears from her face - some from joy, some from sadness. She brought her lips up to the shiny glass window pane and whispered, "I'll miss you, my daughter, but I'm home now. I know you'll miss me, too, but please let me go. You have given me so much comfort and joy. I now let you go to enjoy your years. Please know I am safe and happy with your father and brothers. It is time I get to know them again."

She lifted her fingers to her lips and with a gentle breath sent a kiss of love earthward to her waiting daughter. "Your momma loves you and blesses you."

A gentle wind sent the kiss spiraling down, earthbound, to find and kiss a lonely daughter.

****

And so, my mother made her journey home. I miss her terribly, but she has a loving family and friends to ease her into the new life that awaits her. I am now the one that is alone.

A footnote: I once read that we all have a guardian angel hovering over us. If we concentrate hard enough and often enough, we can feel their presence and can even be told their name. I did this one evening and the name Luther came to me quite suddenly and without prior thought. I may not see him often or talk to him as I should, but Luther, I know, is watching over me until it is time for him to lead me on my journey home.

.......and now I end my stories. I hope you've enjoyed reminiscing with me and perhaps shared a laugh or even a tear with me.

Growing up "way back then" was a marvelous adventure. To this day, we of the neighborhoods where we grew up share a bond that cannot be broken. "Growing up Greek" was an experience I shall always cherish.

Printed in the United States
1516500003BA/1-39